SURVIVAL GARDENING

SURVIVAL GARDENING

John A. Freeman

drawings by
John E. Dille'

John's Press

ACKNOWLEDGEMENTS

First, I wish to thank those gardeners of varied age and experience whose response to my workshops on Survival Gardening encouraged me to write this book.

My appreciation continues to go to the following colleagues and friends who contributed specifically to the early development of it: Dr. John Dille', who did the hand-drawn illustrations, Dr. John Shive, Dr. Wilburn Newcomb, Arla Holroyd, Dena Lucy, and my son-in-law, Carroll Parker.

I am grateful for the widespread coverage in the media and by word of mouth. Enthusiastic and perceptive reviews and articles undoubtedly helped make an early second printing necessary.

However, it was the interested questions and comments made to me personally by individuals struggling to garden under unfavorable conditions over the U.S. that resulted in the decision to do an expanded new edition instead.

Again I wish to thank the personnel at Art Printing Company for their enthusiastic competence.

Especially, I need to recognize my wife, Grace, whose sensitivity to language and whose abilities as editor/designer have left their impress throughout both editions.

Single copies may be ordered prepaid direct from publisher for $8.95 plus $1.00 delivery charge.

JOHN'S PRESS
Box 3405 CRS
Rock Hill, SC 29731
Phone: 803-366-7392

Printed in the United States of America
by Art Printing Company, Inc.

Cover art and design
by Jack Russell and Grace Freeman

ISBN 0-9607730-5-3

To my mother,
who first stimulated my love of and interest in foods

To the memory of my father,
who taught me my first lessons in ecology

To my wife,
who is chief mulcher and soup maker extraordinary

and to our children,
whose interest in gardening blossomed
with families of their own to feed

CONTENTS

J's
P

UPON HALF-VIEWING A FILM ON DROUGHT IN AFRICA

Through thin eye slits,
I manage to view the plight
of zebras, lions and leopards
who seek old water holes
find bowls of dust instead
and are reduced to chalky sculptures
in a gallery of sand.

I have to cheat, not look
at closeup shots of clustering flies
on faces of children paper thin,
too weak to lift their hands.

With my eyes closed, I am aware
that from these bony babies
skeleton mothers clutch tight
there comes no sound at all.
Starving children do not cry,
they only stare.

Grace B. Freeman

From **No Costumes or Masks**
© Red Clay Books, 1975, 1976, 1981

Just in Case ...
A 1000 sq. ft. garden to live on!

*The struggle --
the ceaseless war against
hunger -- is as old
as man himself, and never
has the outcome
been more in doubt.*

International Food
Policy Institute

CHAPTER ONE

The whole modern food system is complex and highly vulnerable to disruption. What will you do if social, economic, political or other forces suddenly decrease availability or skyrocket the costs of the food you and your family consume at great distances from where it is grown? The continued degradation of land and the rapid rise in population also foreshadow a critical food problem within a decade or two, even if favorable growing weather prevails.

Common sense suggests anticipatory steps at family and community levels must be taken quickly as a matter of self-interest and to lessen the impact of foreseeable events. *Survival Gardening* provides the basic information for getting enough nutrition from your home garden to live on . . . just in case!

In this chapter the basis for choosing those vegetables which provide the highest nutrition for the space and time is presented. A typical garden will have its nutritive yield raised by the choices made among alternative vegetables. Measured in terms of a balance of the nutrients humans need, it is reasonable for gardeners to expect a ten-fold increase in yield when the various features of Survival Gardening are adopted.

The aims in Survival Gardening are to meet nutritional needs using a minimum amount of space, to have a reliable means of meeting these requirements, and to develop a sustainable system for doing this.

One requirement for Survival Gardening is reliability of production year after year. Several studies have shown that productivity of organic agriculture is more stable from year to year than conventional farming. Organic farms have, on the average, somewhat lower productivity than

---

Anticipatory Action

This is a very special section where the term Survival Gardening has the most meaning. In it the technic for sharply increasing the *nutrient* yield of *any* garden is given. All of us hope our families never have to depend completely on home gardens for food. On the chance that this may be necessary at some time in the future, here are suggestions for the present:

1. Post a copy of the list of Very Special Survival Vegetables in a reasonable place where you can review as needed.

2. Learn to raise, store, use and perpetuate each of the Very Special Survival Vegetables that will grow in your area.

3. Experiment to find the best varieties of these vegetables for your soil and climate.

4. Maintain a rotating seed stock of V.S.S.V. sufficient for at least two years' planting. These should be carefully protected from pests and kept cool so they retain their viability.

5. Review this most important section of Survival Gardening from time to time and maintain your capability to put its principles into effect if natural or man-made disaster should come.

---

conventional farms but their production in poor years is much higher than that from conventional farms. This reliability is basic in Survival Gardening.

Sustainability of soil productivity has historically been associated with one or more of three factors: seasonal flooding, a balance of animal husbandry and agriculture with manuring, or crop rotation involving legumes and other green manure crops. Most of us cannot take advantage of flooding. Those having minimal area for food production may not have space for animals or may not want to use animals. Even if animals are used, legumes provide the most efficient means of nitrogen fertilizer production.

Thus far the logic is the same as that of any organic, natural, or biodynamic gardening system. The problem arises when we try to meet human nutritional needs completely or almost completely from gardening in a minimal space. In many gardens the produce is fine in meeting mineral and vitamin requirements but is deficient in calories and protein. Then too, a person simply cannot eat enough tomatoes (20 to 30 pounds), lettuce (40 to 60 pounds) or broccoli (18 to 27 pounds) to meet the daily energy requirements.

The table of Very Special Survival Vegetables (p.11) provides a key to meeting human nutritional needs as well as providing a green manure service to nourish the soil.

Two groups of plants have been selected: first, vegetables which provide in good gardening practice on average the highest yields of calories or at least two of the nutrients studied; and second, several legumes which provide human food and also green manure for soil enrichment.

Using the yields per 25 square feet that might be expected of a good gardener (pp.64-66) you can easily work out possible planting schedules to maximize the yields of calories and the five nutrients for which estimates have been made. Thus in one plot Irish potatoes and lettuce might be planted with anticipation of half a crop of lettuce. This could be followed by collards with a half a crop of radishes. The calculated yields for the year for the 25 square feet are:

Calories	Protein (gm)	Calcium (mgm)	Iron (mgm)	Vitamin A (IU)	Vitamin C (mgm)
25,000	1300	51,000	150	1,500,000	8900

Surprisingly, the calories are sufficient for slightly over eight days for a 3000 C per day diet while each other nutrient, on the basis of U.S. standards, is sufficient for an equal or longer period for the average person.

Study of several such projected plantings leads to the conclusion that when a mixed vegetable diet is used, providing a sufficiency of calories is the problem, not, as is commonly assumed, having enough protein. (This is reinforced by the conclusion of United Nations nutrition experts that in many countries people getting enough calories will also have a sufficiency of protein.) Using a mix of the Very Special Survival Vegetables to provide enough calories can assure a person will have enough of each of the indicated nutrients.

The Very Special Survival Vegetables (V.S.S.V.)

Very Special Survival Vegetables	Calories	Protein	Calcium	Iron	Vitamin A	Vitamin C
Beans, lima*		4				
Beans, snap*						
Beets with greens			4	2		
Butterpeas*						
Chard			2	7	4	
Collards	5	7	6		7	4
Garlic	6	4				
Kale		5	3	4	5	3
Mustard		4	4	8	5	3
Parsnips	6					
Peas (various)*						
Potato, Irish	9	4				
Rutabaga	9		3			3
Salsify	6					
Soybeans*	5	5		2		
Spinach		4	2	7	5	
Sweetpotato	6				4	
Turnips with greens	10	10	10	10	10	10

*Legumes

This table provides relative caloric and nutritive yields of common vegetables expected from a good garden per week of growth per unit space. The top producers are rated on a scale of 2 to 10, the latter used to indicate the top yielder and the other figures indicating lower yields by tens of percents. (A vegetable rated 8, for example, on the average in intensive culture would be expected to provide about 80% as much of the indicated dietary component as one rated 10.)

You can use the table to develop a garden plan which will provide the highest yield per week of a particular nutrient or calories. By using a mixture of vegetables, a small amount of food of animal origin, and preferably some whole grains you can have not only an adequate but a very good diet. Legumes, which are important for nitrogen fixation and soil growth, are included even though only two for which calculations have been made, butterbeans and soybeans, produce as much as 20% of the highest yielder per week per unit area.

Several other vegetables are high producers of a single nutrient but not of calories. Such omissions are Jerusalem artichokes (a good protein producer), carrots (high in vitamin A), cucumber, leaf lettuce and radishes (high transmitters of iron).

In all the calculations made thus far, two to three square feet of intensively cultivated plots can each year provide the recommended daily allowance of nutrients for an adult male. Since children and women have lower caloric requirements, it appears safe to conclude that a Survival Garden allotting 1000 square feet per person and cultivated intensively can, except for vitamin B-12 (cobalamine) which almost all plants except comfrey lack, meet the dietary needs of the group. This is especially true if a modest amount of meat, fish, milk, or eggs (or other foods of animal origin) is available to complement the plant protein as well as provide vitamin B-12.

Now the question is, is this a true picture of how we would use Survival Gardening in an emergency? Well, no — not exactly, for several reasons, some of which we can actually turn to our advantage. The first reason it may not be like this simply is that there may be crop failures. Fortunately, complete crop failures are rare in most areas and, except for drought or very excessive rain, it is very unusual for more than one or two crops to fail in any one year. Rather heavy rains are not much of a problem when the raised mounds method of gardening is used. In case rainfall is inadequate the growing areas are small, so the amount of water, if any, needed for irrigation is low. About a gallon per square foot applied directly to the soil each week in the driest weather is sufficient — and except in the hottest weather even this is not required unless there is no rain for several weeks.

... the most valuable of all arts will be ... deriving a comfortable subsistence from the smallest area of soil.

A. Lincoln

One precaution against crop failure from drought is to plant some of the land in milo or sorghum, two grains which have wide ranges of water tolerance. Both are grown extensively for human food in arid areas of Africa though in the U.S. their primary use is for stock feeding.

So much for the unfavorable side. Other variations from the Survival Gardening table can often be used to advantage.

Higher yielding and rapidly producing strains of many vegetables are available. For example, Winter Bloomsdale spinach is a good choice for both these reasons as well as the fact that it is especially cold resistant. Cylindra beets are a good choice since the yield is about double that of other varieties. Two varieties of Irish potatoes may differ in time to maturity by three weeks — enough to have a three-season rather than two-season garden in some places.

Advantage can also be taken of space vacated. For example, collards may be planted just at the outer leaftips of potatoes that will be dug in a week or ten days. Presoaked beans or butterpeas can be planted where turnips are being pulled. With easily worked soil even small spaces can be reworked and reused so the growing space is occupied a very high fraction of the gardening season.

The ideal to be worked toward is having a steady supply of fresh vegetables during the growing season with reasonable amounts for drying and canning. Winter needs can be met partially using dried or canned foods but the fall garden should provide several vegetables including turnips, rutabagas, collards, parsnips and salsify which can be harvested as needed during the winter in less frigid areas and, along with Irish potatoes and sweetpotatoes, can be stored for several months in a cool place.

Additional technics discussed elsewhere that can intensify use of space include presoaking seeds a day or so before planting or actually germinating them between moist papers, starting plants in paper cups, flower pots, flats or coldframes for later transplanting, and provision of fencing or poles for appropriate plants to grow on. Considering transplanting as an example, a good plan is to keep a few plants on hand so fresh ones can be inserted as space becomes available. After all, you may need to

It is highly probable that among the countless plants people in other cultures grow many would meet or even exceed the nutritive productivity of those in this first listing of Very Special Survival Vegetables. Most will undoubtedly be from the plant-rich Orient. As additional information becomes available, the list will be modified.

J.A.F.

harvest only one plant at a time if collecting collards, rutabaga or Irish potatoes. So plantings of only four or five plants at first, followed by single insertions at frequent intervals, can be an effective way to assure a steady harvest most suited to the immediate needs of your family.

Another unreal assumption in the illustration is plantings of twenty-five square feet. Under normal circumstances for two persons you would not plant over 10 square feet in spinach or five in beets at any one time, preferring, rather, several small plantings. On the other hand, much more extensive plantings of sources of more concentrated energy, such as Irish potatoes, sweetpotatoes, corn, soybeans and limas, are appropriate.

You will recall that the Survival Garden is to nourish not only people but the soil itself. Hence the gardening plan includes legumes in an interplanting or rotating scheme. For this purpose, as well as for human food, some legumes should be planted, preferably covering perhaps 25 to 35 percent of the garden at some time each year.

Yet another option in warmer areas is to plant a legume cover crop in the fall in part of the garden, changing areas each year. Broadbeans can be used for this in some areas. Snowpeas and English peas can be used similarly but more widely.

Many vegetables are harvested over a period of days or weeks. In the case of snapbeans, for example, the first several pickings may not provide enough for a meal. But then comes a period of weeks in which a 15 square foot area produces all two persons can eat plus some to preserve. Then there is a week or so of diminishing production. A second planting that dovetails with the first so the two harvests overlap makes good sense.

Surviving On 1000 Square Feet Per Person

The average person requires about 900,000 calories per year. The garden plan shown on p. 67, well done, is expected to provide about 850,000 calories per year on not over 1000 square feet of growing surface. If, on the other hand, the maximum production figures of Jeavons are used as indicated in his book, *"How to Grow More Vegetables..."*, there is the hypothetical production of 1.8 million calories, or well more than the maximum required per human being.

The plan for Survival Gardening was developed on the assumption that the limit would be set by calorie production. To test this assumption, calculations of protein and a number of minerals and vitamins produced in this hypothetical garden were made and gave the following results: Protein available from the garden is about 1.7 times the average RDA for this nutrient; calcium, iron, thiamin, riboflavin and niacin range between 2.4 and 5.4 times the average RDA; vitamin A is 13 times and vitamin C a "whopping" 23 times the RDA. These values are high enough that typical losses during food preparation or storage would not be critical.

Since any person striving for complete food self-sufficiency will probably plan to have some food from non-garden sources, the produce of this garden should be sufficient. For example, one might easily have the following available even on a city lot:

Honey	100 pounds	138,000 Calories
Pecans	100 pounds	165,000 Calories
Walnuts	50 pounds	31,000 Calories

The honey or the pecans can more than make up the difference between the anticipated production of the postulated garden and the average recommended caloric intake. In case you are worried about the high sugar intake using this much honey, it amounts to only 60% of present average American sugar consumption. It would, in fact, be below average sugar consumption at any time in the 20th Century.

*No unemployment insurance
can be compared to
an alliance between
man and a plot of land.*

Henry Ford

There are, however, several problems with the survival diet assumed here. It is certainly quite different from the diet to which most Americans are accustomed and would require some "getting used to." The volume of food is unusually high for Americans. It would seem monotonous but can be made more attractive with herbs for seasoning and teas. Using some additional ground for a few vegetables raised primarily for taste and texture, as tomatoes, peppers, okra, cucumbers, melons and squash, would help. Rabbits and/or chickens could add variety to the diet and could help the calorie/weight ratio. Cooperation with someone with a cow or milk goat could provide milk, cheese and meat.

Another possibility for the transition period during which intensification of gardening occurs is use of stored foods such as whole grains, powdered milk, dried foods and canned goods. In fact, anyone planning for food self-sufficiency will need to develop a food storage plan and this is more easily done prior to rather than at the time of need. Recalling The Depression -- the last time many families experienced the need for self-sufficiency -- some of you will remember it as a character molding experience but not a time of real hunger. Shelf after shelf of canned goods -- food raised in home garden, orchard, poultry yard, fencerow or pasture -- saw to that. Each fall fortunate people living in the country had enough in the cupboard to carry their families through a couple of years.

Perhaps here the point is that it is important to have not only gardening skills but other basic survival skills and attitudes and to conduct life in the present in anticipation of what may or may not come in the future. Such an anticipatory life can be joyous and voluntary, not a condition to avoid. As far as food is concerned, the ideal anticipatory action would be community-wide work toward sufficiency in production, processing and storage, especially of the Very Special Survival Vegetables. In critical times, whether of short duration or permanent, such a development in both family and community could make the difference between tragedy and survival with dignity.

Site Selection ...

Pick a place in the sun

*We abuse land because
we regard it as a commodity
belonging to us.
When we see land as a
community to which we belong,
we may begin to use it
with love and respect.*

Aldo Leopold

CHAPTER TWO

For some of you, site selection may simply mean using the space you have. For those who have enough space that choice among several sites is practical, it is an important matter. A general biological principle is that a limit is finally set by *one* condition, such as temperature or moisture or a nutrient or some other factor. Even so, a series of conditions must all be met if a garden is to be successful. Site selection is for the purpose of optimizing gardening possibilities for a particular area.

The single most critical item for Survival Gardening is choosing an area that receives full sunlight several hours per day — preferably six or eight or more — during the major growing season. A very few garden vegetables thrive in partial shade and a few herbs do best in partial shade but most will produce poorly unless subject to bright sunlight for several hours daily.

It is easy to diminish the hours of exposure to direct sunlight but, unfortunately, increasing sunlight exposure often involves a choice we do not want to make, such as trimming or even cutting down a favorite tree or shrub. However, a particular site should always be examined to see if changes could be made to provide sunlight. If trees and shrubs shade a potential garden spot, it is possible some relandscaping would be practical and even profitable.

If relandscaping is chosen, consider several alternative ideas. Should the change be effected quickly or over a period of some years? To what uses will the non-garden area that is left be put? What types of plants should be used? Are structures, such as arborways, to be used instead of trees? Will the possibilities of providing some fruit or for attracting wildlife, especially birds, be considered?

One whose garden space is already sunlit is fortunate but developing ideas for modifying a yard using the above and other questions will present an interesting challenge to those who need to open up their potential garden space to the light.

Light-wise, an even greater challenge may be faced by those whose land is shaded by trees growing on the property of someone else. Cooperation may be possible and the opportunity for a community garden may be an attractive alternative to be explored.

The second most crucial site choice basis is soil — second, because in the Survival Gardening method one builds soil and this can be done on any piece of ground though obviously it is much easier if a reasonably rich soil serves as a starting point. If weeds grow well in an area, it will also support many vegetables. If weeds do not grow for some obvious reason — the area is in a chicken yard; it is too shaded; the soil is very acid or very alkaline, etc. — the fact of no weeds does not necessarily mean the soil is hopeless.

In any case, an otherwise promising site should be examined carefully to determine if any easily remedied factors are preventing usual growth of weeds or grass. If the texture of the soil is fairly good, indicating a mixture of clay, silt and sand, then it will probably be relatively easy to correct deficiencies, given some time and effort.

Slope is a third consideration. A slight slope to the south for air drainage is ideal. Except for a slight slope, such as a foot or two in 50 feet, the greater the slope the more unfavorable the site. Even very steep slopes can be terraced, as has been done extensively in Peru, Java, China and other areas. For gardening, it is best if the terraces can be oriented basically east-west, unless they are to correct for only slight differences in elevation.

A problem in soils that is less widespread than in the past is waterlogging — soils in some spots too moist for most plants. Seepage areas where the water table is very near or at the surface is the usual cause of waterlogging but the lowering of water tables as we have partially depleted our underground water resources has resulted in a sharp decrease in waterlogging. However, the unintentional cure of the problem is more serious than the "disease".

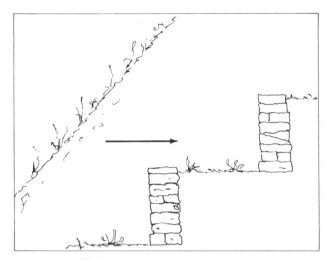

Even a steep hillside can be terraced to accommodate vegetables.

The Survival Gardening technic of using elevated beds should solve the waterlogging problem in almost every case. However, if there is some natural slope, drainage onto a lawn or other planted area can be provided and usually will remedy the situation. Yet another possibility is to take advantage of the over-moist condition by growing watercress or various mints.

An area in which there is adequate air drainage (cold air flowing down) and protected on the north or northwest side is important in spring and fall since frost damage is less likely than in cold pockets with little air movement.

Primary consideration so far has been given to site selection by persons having relatively restricted areas for gardens. If you have lots of room, you may want to consider placing your garden in a mixed ecosystem that will maintain populations of various predators that will help keep insects, snails, slugs, mice, etc. under control. Having such predators working for you instead of having their prey working against you is a big boon. (For further ideas see pp. 47-53.)

Once you have decided where to put your garden you will have a use for tools.

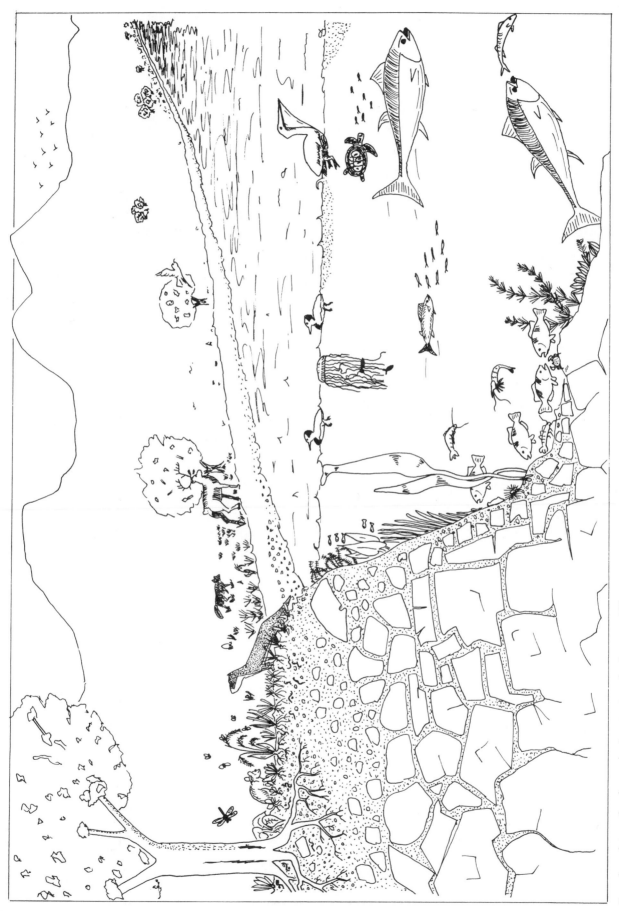

Organisms interacting in a mixed ecosystem develop a stability which can be shared by a garden.

I farm
the soil that yields my food
I share creation.
Kings can do no more.

Ancient Chinese poem

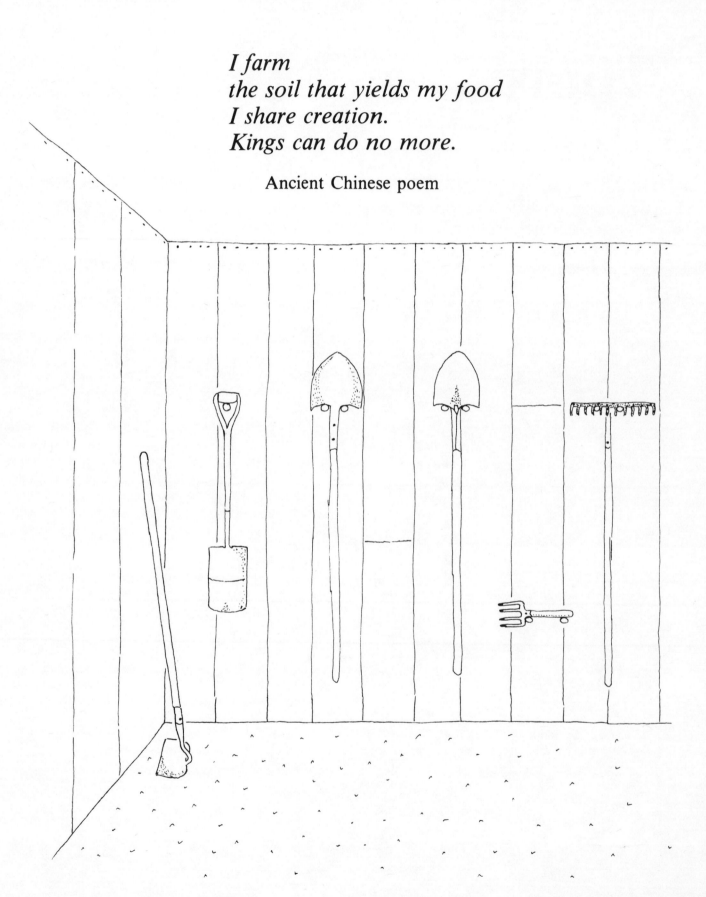

Tools ...
The right ones for you

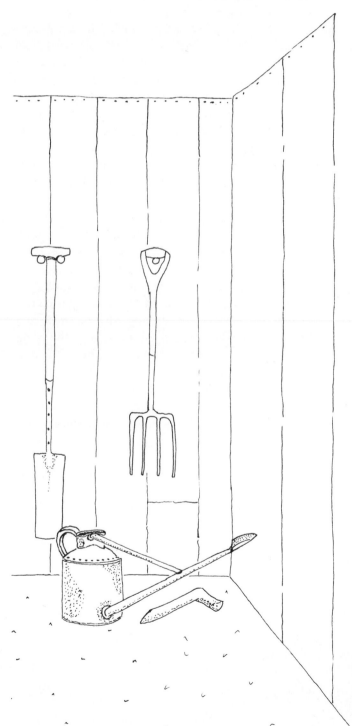

CHAPTER THREE

Although the tools needed for Survival Gardening are pretty minimal, the specific choice is highly important both in terms of types of tools and quality.

However, if you already have tools — perhaps even a garden tractor, tiller, and leaf and limb grinder — by all means use them in the early stages in preparation of your garden on a new site. It will be easier with power tools than with hand tools. In fact, if you do not have power tools, you may want to start off renting a rotary tiller or paying someone to till the soil the first time around. However, this certainly is not necessary, especially if you are changing over from conventional gardening. If you are already gardening, change part of your garden the first year and more the next. If you are a beginner, start small and gradually build up to your final size. If you start in an off season, as late fall or early winter, mulch the area heavily to let nature help in the original preparation.

Now the tools you will need. The first is a shovel or a spade. Considerable emotion can develop between proponents of shovels and spades, long and short handles. Whichever you decide on, select the best you can find. They will have either a "solid" shank (the wooden handle fits into the metal shank) or a two-strapped shank rather than an open socket (constructed as though wrapped partway around the handle). It is best to "heft" a number of them to find substantial tools that fit your size and feel right to you. If you own several, you may find your preference changes from job to job. A heavy shovel may be just right for heavy digging; a smaller and lighter one, for most transplanting. You may use two simultaneously, especially when moving rather large plants or when moving compost or manure. In the former case, you may dig the hole with one shovel and with the other move the plant in a shovelful of soil. The first shovel is then used to fill the hole around the plant before removing the supporting shovel. If moving compost, manure or soil, you may want one shovel for filling the cart and the other for whatever is done where it is unloaded.

A good hoe is the second tool, a quality farm hoe with a good, comfortable handle. Select a hoe in which the blade and bent rod that attaches it to the handle are of unit construction rather than spot welded or soldered.

A posthole shovel — a very long-bladed shovel — and a posthole digger will occasionally come in handy.

A garden fork with 4 to 6 tines is very useful, especially for loosening the subsoil in double digging. It is also good for digging potatoes and in a pinch can substitute for a pitchfork when only a little use is anticipated.

A metal rake, with tines about 3 inches long, rounds out the list of important larger hand tools for working the soil.

Now for the smaller ones. A garden trowel with a comfortable handle is important for transplanting.

Several other hand tools are convenient to have in addition to the trowel. A dibble, simply a pointed stick for making holes for small, bare-root transplants, is easily made from a limb or from a foot-long section of a broom handle. A dwarf rake and hoe corresponding in size with the trowel are useful at times, especially in transplanting.

One of the most useful "tools" for the garden and elsewhere is a cart with two over-sized ball-bearing wheels. Kits for several sizes are available.

Tools are so important in gardening and can last so long that it is wise to buy only good ones. They often cost more but spread over many years of service and not needing frequent replacement, they probably cost less in the long run. It is better to buy fewer tools, spread out purchases, or look for good tools second-hand than to settle for inferior equipment.

An important aspect of tools is their care. It is well to go past the obvious avoidance of leaving tools out in the rain or dirty. If the handle is not varnished, a "seasoning" with a linseed oil, turpentine mixture (2:1), applied and rubbed daily for several days, will provide adequate protection for wooden handles, which may also be varnished. Blades should be cleaned after use and the metal worked through oiled sand in a small barrel or large bucket. Paint the cart with a high grade outdoor paint such as is sold for deck floors. All tools should be kept dry under shelter when not in use.

Such care pays, for tools can last a lifetime and can even be passed on from generation to generation.

Now that you have your garden site selected and the tools to get the space ready for planting, it's time to decide what to grow.

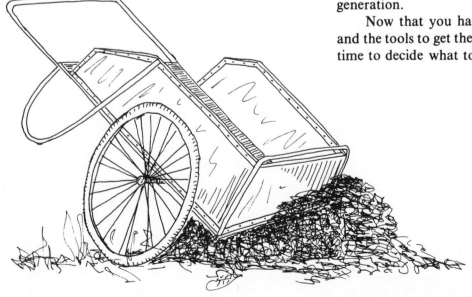

What to Grow ...
A look at some basics

*... the earth bringeth forth
fruit of herself;
first the blade, then the ear,
after that the full corn
in the ear.*

The Gospel of Mark

CHAPTER FOUR

There is more to this section on what to grow than first meets the eye. It is obvious that certain crops do well in any particular area -- after all, "everyone" grows them. Such an observation provides a starting list and suggests the question: What *else* will grow here? A bit of enquiry and you may find that many vegetables, fruits and herbs will grow in your area but, in fact, are seldom raised there.

So, especially if for the present you are gardening for the fun of it and to provide your own fresh vegetables and certain herbs and spices that are otherwise not available to you, you may want to let your list grow, possibly outlandishly. If you can grow a few things away from where they normally thrive, then you can certainly grow the ordinary!

It is time, however, to look at some basics. You now have a list of sorts. How do you choose from the wide variety of species or types on your list?.

Consider four bases for choices: Vegetables that will grow in your area and will fit the space available are essentials, certainly, and you want to consider the taste tickling qualities of your produce, too. But nutritional value, which is often overlooked, is equally important.

In making choices on the basis of nutritional value the U.S.D.A. *Handbook Number 8* or another source of such information is a "must". It lists the nutritive values of most fruits, vegetables and other primary foods and of many prepared ones. Protein, minerals and key vitamins, fats and caloric values are given in lengthy tables.

Considering a great deal of data on nutrition as well as some other factors, this list, developed for a course in Survival Gardening, is as follows: Beans and peas (especially string beans, lima beans, butterpeas, soybeans and snow peas), the cole plants

*Green leaves
are the largest producers
of protein in the world.*
Medard Gabel

(broccoli, Brussel sprouts, cabbage, collards, etc.), spinach, kale, Swiss chard, tomatoes, carrots, green peppers, squashes, radishes, lettuce, sweet and Irish potatoes, corn and muskmelon. Eggplant and cucumbers may be on your personal list because you like them. Easily grown, both add taste and texture variety to the diet. For most people, onions would be listed for a similar reason. Turnips, beets, rutabaga, salsify, parsnips, and Jerusalem artichokes may be added, primarily because they keep well for use in winter. Comfrey could be added as a source of Vitamin B-12 or at the seashore you might use seaweeds.

This list, of course, is too long for a beginner, Narrow it by considering whether each will grow well in your area. Other than trial and error, which a beginning gardener should try to avoid, you have four sources of information on this. The most useful source is the gardening publications. Each state has an Agricultural Extension Service from which valuable pamphlets can be obtained. The local Agriculture Extension Agent or the state landgrant college will have these on hand. Gardening columns, often reflecting a high level of information, can be found in newspapers and regional magazines. And there are more books on gardening than anyone will have time for, regional ones often being most helpful.

Stores dealing in farm supplies can provide information on local plant choices and are very valuable in this respect as well as being sources of seed, equipment and other gardening supplies.

Local gardeners are almost invariably delighted to discuss gardening, and often have information on local conditions that is hard to obtain elsewhere.

Next, consider how to coordinate your garden with other foods available now or especially in an emergency. Among considerations may be what vegetables you commonly obtain locally, whether by purchase, gift, or exchange.

If your emergency storage includes whole grains (wheat, oats, corn, rice), soybeans, peas, and dried milk, kept in tightly closed metal or glass containers, you do not presently need to emphasize protein and calories in foods from your garden. So you may not want to raise beans and peas and potatoes in very large quantities. Such logic will allow you to refine your list further.

Finally, consider space. If you need the maximum nutrition possible or you want to maximize one or two special nutrients, consult the chapter on the Very Special Survival Vegetables (pp. 9-14).

Look at the space requirements for particular plants. Parsley, which is very vitamin rich, requires little space. Peppers, cabbage, broccoli, and tomatoes (if staked) require moderate amounts of space.

Single plants can be grown, if need be. However, a single plant of string beans, butter beans or any of the peas makes no sense, so you will need to devote 15 to 25 square feet to these (somewhat less if pole varieties are chosen). Corn can be hand pollinated but ordinarily the absolute minimum area for corn is 25 to 30 square feet.

(Note: In considering space, see the chapter on planting and the table on p. 69. Most garden plants can be grown much closer together in the intensive culture of Survival Gardening than in usual agricultural practice.)

With the ideas discussed above, plus details on spacing from p. 69, you are ready to further refine your planting list. For a small space, yet big enough as a start for a small family of four, try two 3 x 20 foot plots. Your list at this point might be something like this: tomatoes, carrots, lettuce, okra, cabbage, radish, parsley, green peppers, summer squash and lima beans.

Next use the table on p. 74 to find the approximate area required per plant and to determine the total area needed for your family, if you plant the vegetables listed in minimal amounts. Successional plantings and interplantings will, in effect, extend the space you have but need not be considered at this point. The idea here is simply to ask if you might reasonably use the list developed in planting a garden this size.

There is a final step — and this may be the most fun of all in planning a garden: selecting the special varieties to be grown.

There are many varieties of some vegetables, such as tomatoes and cabbages, but very few of others, such as okra, kohlrabi and Swiss chard. In some cases, the varieties differ in very significant ways. Others are so similar that the choice is simply a matter of personal preference.

Another occupation in February is hunting for the first sign of spring.
Carel Capek

The information you need for selecting among the varieties available will come primarily from three sources. Your local seedsman can tell you which varieties he sells thrive in your area. The Agricultural Extention Service has pamphlets providing similar information. Fortunately these are updated as field trials show new varieties are suited to particular areas. In addition, careful reading of seed catalogs will provide essential information on choices of varieties. And, of course, your own taste buds will be stimulated by what you have been given by enthusiastic gardening friends or you have purchased at a local source.

The seed catalogs can both steer you from inappropriate varieties and lead you to ones best suited to your needs as a home gardener. Consider the following varietal descriptions in several catalogs:

Remarkable disease resistance	Ideal market size
Good crops under adverse conditions	Excellent shipper
	Commands good price
Flavor superb	Uniform ripening
Excellent for home use	Very prolific
Excellent quality	Uniform maturity
Old reliable	Heavy yielder
In edible condition very long	

The two lists reveal good things about the particular varieties but in general the list on the left provides more signals indicating suitability to the needs of home gardeners. In certain situations the Survival Gardener, however, will want to choose items having characteristics in the right hand column. Specifically, if you plan to preserve, whether by drying, freezing, canning or pickling, you may give preference to certain varieties that ripen mostly all at once. For day to day use, however, an extended season is better. Likewise, if food supplies are low or are expected to be low one season you are justified in selecting heavy yielding varieties. Fortunately, there are varieties of many vegetables that combine characteristics in the left column with heavy yielding.

*The earth
has yielded its increase;
God, our God, has blessed us.*
Psalm 67

Some varieties have shorter growing periods and so may make more efficient use of space. This factor should be considered especially in regions of short growing seasons or for interim or fall plantings.

Another consideration is that some varieties have higher nutrient yields than others of the same type. Thus green, leafy lettuces and deep-colored pumpkins, squashes and sweetpotatoes are better sources of vitamins than their less colorful counterparts and new varieties of carrots, tomatoes and other vegetables are coming along featuring high nutritive values.

Choice of varieties completes this preliminary planning except for deciding how much seed or how many plants to purchase. Additional information in the chapter on planting and especially information on spacing and seed needs, pp. 69 and 73, will help you decide this. If this is your first garden, you will probably be safe getting a single packet of each type of seed. In fact, you and a neighbor may be able to share a packet of each type of seed.

If you purchase seed from a farm supply store you may be able to buy them weighed out. The price is usually lower and you can obtain the amount of seed you need with less waste.

Should you use the hybrids? Yes and no. If you need to raise the most food in the least space and with the least work this season, hybrids are often a good choice. If you anticipate being a true Survival Gardener and saving your own seed, all of which is covered in Chapter Ten, pp. 59-62, then dependence on hybrids is definitely not for you. Hybrids don't breed true, usually producing only inferior plants the second year.

As to when to order seeds, catalogs usually arrive about the time one feels really housebound in the winter. Spirits rise as you pore over them. Ordering soon after the catalogs arrive assures the seeds will be on hand when you have the soil prepared.

A thing is right when it tends to preserve the integrity, stability and beauty of the biotic community. It is wrong when it tends otherwise.
Aldo Leopold

Soil Buildup ...

Getting ready to plant

Earth and water,
if not blatantly abused,
can be made to produce
again and again
for the benefit of all.
The key is wise stewardship.
Stewart L. Udall

CHAPTER FIVE

Soil preparation and building is one of the most important phases of Survival Gardening. The general purpose is to develop the best soil possible from what nature, ignorance, perhaps avarice and almost certainly neglect have provided, for it is this thin layer that supports all land life, including our own.

The desired soil has all those good characteristics that help plants grow and flourish — good texture, high water holding capacity, a balance of minerals, and a wide variety of organisms including microbes, earthworms and others. For optimum plant growth, the topsoil needs to be deep, much deeper than typical American soils now. And the places where plants are to grow need to be easily accessible to the gardener and yet arranged so the soil will not be compacted around the roots during work or harvest.

The general plan to bring about these good purposes is to do your gardening in small, raised plots with walkways between. Experienced gardeners will find this rather easily accomplished when they convert from the usual gardening methods to Survival Gardening. Many gardeners may want to change gardening technics slowly over a period of years. The following instructions are primarily for new or relatively inexperienced gardeners, for experienced gardeners would need less detail.

First, either with stakes or in your mind, lay out the area to be used, including walk-space all around. A convenient area is about five to six feet wide (the east-west dimension, if level and otherwise practical) and 15 to 20 feet long, which will provide a garden about three by twelve to seventeen feet or so — probably half enough for a beginner, depending on your enthusiasm and vigor.

If recommendations based on a soil analysis are available, follow them for soil additives such as manure, compost, agricultural lime or dolomite. (For a detailed method of calculating organic equivalents of commercial fertilizer recommendations see Chapter Eleven, pp. 74-75. If, like most, you are anxious to plant before your soil analysis is available, spread about three inches of compost or well-rotted leaves or sawdust or manure over the garden before digging for planting. If you do not have this much, spread what you do have.

Maximum amounts of the following manures per 100 square feet for loamy soil are:

Cattle, fresh	50 lbs.
Cattle, dry	18 lbs.
Horse, fresh	50 lbs.
Sheep, dry	10 lbs.
Chicken, fresh	28 lbs.
Chicken, dry	10 lbs.

If you live where soils are somewhat acid, this is a good time to spread a quart or so of wood ashes, agricultural lime, dolomite or basic slag per 100 square feet.

Before starting to dig, check to see if the soil has an appropriate moisture content — a fist-ball should crumble on pressure if it is a loam. For digging, use a shovel or spade, as you prefer.

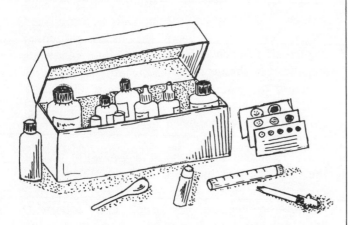

Soil organic matter is one of our most important national resources ...
USDA Agriculture Yearbook, 1938

Hand Tests for Soil Type

	Sand	Sandy loam	Loam	Clay loam	Clay
Gritty	4	3	2	1	0
Sticky if wet	-	-	-	1	3
Dirties hand	-	1	2	3	4

Key: Numbers indicate relative degrees of indicated characteristics.

Hand Tests for Soil Moisture Content

Soil moisture	Sand	Sandy loam	Loam	Clay loam	Clay
		Soil Type			
Too little	1,2	1,2	1,2	1	1,3
Barely enough	1	1,4	1,4,5	1,5	7,8
Enough	4 4	5	6	6	7,8
Plenty	5 9	6,9	6,9	6,9	7,8,9
Too much	10	7,10	7,10	7,10	7,10

Key to soil characteristics:

1 Appears dry
2 Will flow through fingers
3 "Baked"; surface may be cracked or crumbly
4 Can not be formed into ball
5 May form into weak ball
6 Forms into ball that will break on pressure
7 Forms into ball that will not break on pressure
8 Can be formed into ribbon; surface slick
9 No free water released on pressure; hands moist when soil is squeezed
10 Water will drain off or appear on surface when pressed

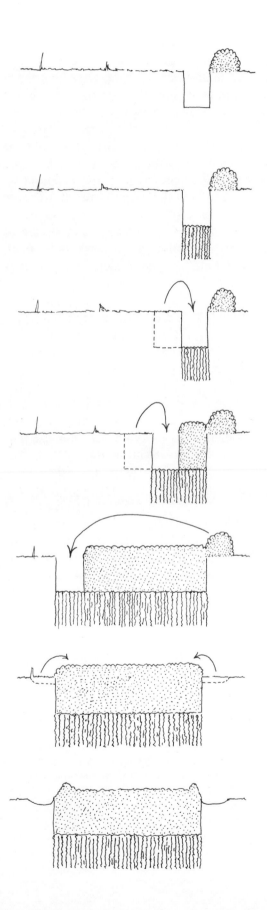

Start at one end of the plot and remove soil one-shovel-deep or to the subsoil, whichever is less. As the soil is removed, throw it into a pile at the end of the plot, removing sticks, stones, glass, clinkers, or other undesireable materials as you work.

The first trenching should be continued to form a ditch across the plot and about two feet wide. The next step is to loosen the subsoil. This may be done with a shovel but is best accomplished with a sturdy pronged digger shaped and used as a spade. Force the shovel or digger as deeply as possible into the soil at the bottom of the trench and move the handle back and forth to loosen the soil. Repeat until the whole exposed area is loosened enough to let some topsoil get down and new plant roots penetrate.

After this operation is completed, another trench is dug adjacent to the first. This is done exactly as the first except that the removed soil is placed in the previous trench. As before, it is important to remove stones and other undesirable materials.

The process is repeated — alternating trench-digging and subsoil loosening — until the whole plot has been worked over. The result is a long mound running the length of the developing garden with a ditch across one end. The soil removed in the beginning is now added to the mound.

If there are clods, these are best relegated to the bottom of the soil mass or to the slopes. In time, with weathering, tilling, root and earthworm action they will be incorporated into the soil. This is a good time to shape the outer wall of the path if another garden is not to be developed immediately adjacent to this one. The sides should slope gently down to the future path. The soil removed in this step is added to the mound.

At this time, it is extremely important that roots and other plant parts be removed as thoroughly as reasonable. Such weeds as Johnson grass, nutgrass, blackberries, dock, Bermuda grass, honeysuckle and poke need to be dealt with this way. Most other plants encountered in the Carolinas' Piedmont at least offer no great problem for Survival Gardening the way they do in conventional gardening. Some weeds are delicate enough that a bit of cultivation kills them and these and others can not develop through a mulch. Among thriving vegetables, some weeds simply can not compete.

The next step is to redistribute the soil to form a flat-topped mound surrounded by a sunken path. Generally the top of the mound will be rectangular, perhaps 30 inches to three feet wide and 12 to 15 or so feet long. Beds should be narrow enough you can reach at least to the center while standing comfortably in the path. Use narrower mounds for plants growing on a fence or stakes. The general range is two to five feet wide.

After the general form of the mound is developed, use a hoe or rake to smooth the surface and to raise a slight wall of soil to form a dam about an inch or two high completely surrounding the level planting surface of the mound. This is a good time to work some thoroughly rotted manure, sawdust, leaves or other organic materials (compost) into the top several inches of the growing surface, especially if the soil is deficient in humus or in nitrogen.

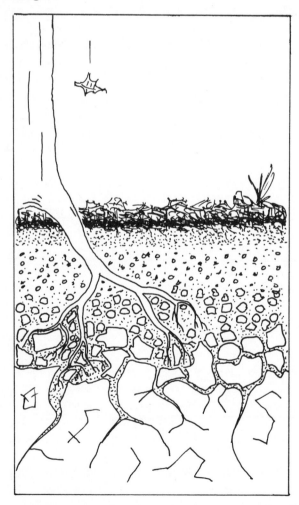

The final step can be taken before or after planting and is most easily done after planting if transplants are used since then it can be combined with immediate mulching of the planting surface. This final step is adding a mulch of leaves, straw or grass clippings to cover the mound slopes and the walkway around the garden. This mulch not only protects the slopes from erosion and evaporation and feeds the earthworms but facilitates decomposition of clods on the slope, makes a composting area of the walkway, and decreases compaction from walking. An especially thick mulch in the path so that mulching material is always on hand for use is a real convenience.

The first garden is now ready for planting. If you are not ready to plant within a day or so, cover the whole planting surface and sides with a mulch and let it sit. If you have a good stock of earthworms and bacteria, they will improve the soil while it waits. If soil preparation is in the fall and the mulched garden stands over winter, you will probably find you can easily rake away the remaining mulch onto the path for later use and then plant before your neighbors do.

If you have space you plan to add to your garden a year or two hence and have a good supply of leaves or old sawdust, mulch this area heavily so that soil building will occur during the interim before the area is used. A soil test and initiation of correction of pH or mineral deficiencies will mean better gardening when the time comes. (See pp. 74-77.)

In nature, plant and animal remains fall to the ground, decay and contribute to humus formation. In their breakdown, organic materials contribute to the chemical processes of weathering, releasing minerals from soil particles. Developing roots contribute to the breaking of rock into soil particles and bring nutrients from deeper levels. In mature ecosystems all wastes are recycled, holding the minerals tightly in a dynamic balance.

Planting ...

Now the fun begins

*If the people work hard
then the earth won't be lazy.*
Peter Chan

CHAPTER SIX

What to plant is treated in two other chapters. Planting is considered here under these subdivisions: when to plant, how to plant, and what to plant together.

Just when to plant particular vegetables depends on the soil temperature and moisture, expected growing conditions (including weather and day lengths), and characteristics of the varieties chosen. Any particular type will germinate and develop well only under a limited range of conditions. Some can tolerate a broad range of environmental situations; others are more restricted in their requirements. Among the environmental factors that must be considered are temperature of the soil, its moisture and, for proper maturation, length of day. While there is a continuous spectrum of plants, for example, from very cold-tolerant to very cold-intolerant, for practical purposes plants are divided into only a few groups with respect to temperature tolerance. Plants within the groups are similar enough that they may all be planted at the same time and usually all will develop.

Since temperature and precipitation vary so much from year to year in many areas, there may be considerable uncertainty as to the best planting dates. For example, you may have had over the years as much as six weeks' difference in the earliest time you succeeded with tomatoes and several weeks variation in the first successful plantings of okra. Because of such variations, for tender crops you may do well to delay planting until even a bit later than the charts indicate. With gardening experience, you will eventually find the optimum time for planting your favorite vegetables and discover that most years your first plantings will be successful. To improve your performance, however, you may want to consider some specifics.

Clay soil is sometimes spoken of as cold, and sandy soil as warm. The reason is that in the spring clay soils heat up more slowly and sandy soils warm up more rapidly. It is logical, therefore, in the spring to plant sandy areas first, if you have a choice.

South-facing slopes in the northern hemisphere receive more solar heat than north-facing ones. Two nearby gardens may, because of this factor alone, need to be planted a week or more apart.

An area protected on the north or northwest by a wall or by trees is warmer than an unprotected area. Further, the wall may retain heat which moderates cooling near it.

You should obtain pamphlets from the local Agricultural Extension Service office for tables on planting times based on studies in your area. Until you are experienced you will do well to follow the instructions carefully as far as planting times are concerned. Page 70 provides information on this.

For Survival Gardening there are three distinct planting patterns and two general methods of planting. These are intended to provide optimum spacing of plants for food production and to use the space to best advantage.

Since Chapter Eleven provides such details as when to plant, spacing, seed depth and numbers of seed to be used, this discussion will deal mainly with general planting principles.

Planting is much easier and quicker if ahead of time the soil has been well developed. Spring planting goes best if the ground has been prepared in late fall, before winter rains, and thoroughly mulched. During warmer spells in winter the earthworms can work the soil, incorporating some of the mulch into it and doing all the other nice things these creatures do free for gardeners. Soil thus prepared is far superior to newly dug plots.

The several general planting patterns are as follows: in hills, in rows, or multiple rows, broadcast in bands and in intermix planting or overlapping combinations of these.

Some plants require enough space that individual plants or small groups are raised in widely spaced spots or hills. Pumpkins, squashes, cucumbers, muskmelons and other vines are planted this way, often in hills four to perhaps eight feet apart, the largest ones in square or triangular patterns or rows.

Naturally, in the small, intensive garden, the largest of the plants mentioned above are usually inappropriate. However, by considering some extra space, possibly lawn, as temporarily part of your garden even the largest pumpkins or far-ranging types of squash or cucumbers may be grown.

Four Planting Patterns

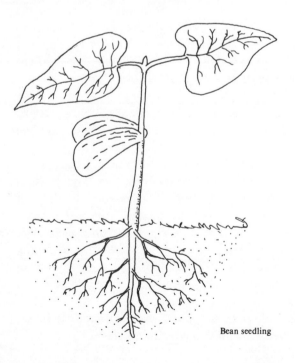

Bean seedling

Broadcast

Hills can be developed as individual mounds built in the manner discussed under Soil Buildup (pp. 25-28) or a mound can be substituted for a series of hills. In the former case, more-or-less round or square mounds are developed that are perhaps three feet in each direction. A generous helping of manure, compost, or rotted sawdust or leaves is dug into the center planting zone. Seeds are then planted in a loose cluster in this area. Care should be taken that the concavity of the planting surface is maintained so that any rain soaks into the mound rather than running off. The soil should then be lightly tamped with a hoe to compact it around the seeds planted, of course, at the proper depths.

When very vigorous-growing vegetables such as squash are planted, a thin, loose mulch of straw, grass clippings or small leaves can be placed directly over the planted surface. A thicker layer, conserving more moisture, should cover the remainder of the mound and also the surrounding path. Some hilled plants grow well on fences or trellised with a significant saving of space. Among these are tomatoes and vine varieties of squash, cucumbers, and muskmelons.

Multiple rows are useful for large and intermediate plants that grow well when fairly closely spaced and the idea can be applied well for those requiring large spacings. The pattern is especially applicable to plants which are big enough to be treated as individuals — peppers, potatoes, cabbages, eggplants, broccoli and even, at times, plants such as lettuce and kohlrabi.

The idea is to provide the required growing space for each plant with the leaves just touching (in most cases) at maturity. The plants in the mound are in rows but staggered in adjacent rows so that more can be grown in a given space with plants the required distance apart.

Many excellent gardeners maintain the best method for spacing out plants is "by eye". Even beginners can try this rather than depend on exact measurements. You will find the measurements are merely approximations anyway and that it quickly becomes second nature to space out plants relatively evenly.

The easiest way to transplant is to dig individual holes with a trowel or shovel in the desired pattern and insert the plants, preferably with some soil attached. Most plants should be planted a bit deeper than in the starting bed, tamped in, watered and then thoroughly mulched. (For ideas on prestarting and overwintering plants for your Survival Garden, see pp. 34-35.)

The same idea fits the planting of beans, okra, late tomatoes, and other seed plants. Or you may want to run furrows either across or lengthwise of the planting area, making neighboring furrows about 8/10ths as far apart as the final distance

Hills

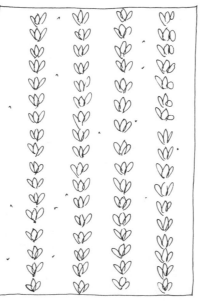

Rows

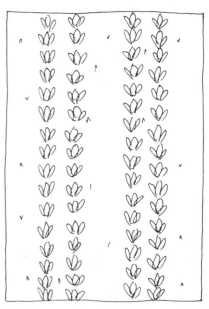

Double Rows

*If ... the earth
cultivates itself naturally,
there is no need for a plow.*
Masanaku Fukuoka

between the mature plants. The seed, individually in the case of larger seeds or in small groups for smaller ones, are dropped into place in two or more rows alternately.

You can plant a few extra seeds of longer-bearing plants, such as okra, that you can then transplant to fill in for ones that do not germinate or for some reason do not thrive. In the case of beans and peas, the plants spread enough to fill in occasional spaces. When several seed are planted together, as with tomatoes, cabbage, broccoli, etc., pull out or transplant all seedlings except the most vigorous one at each spot.

To save time, treat many plants as groups rather than as individuals. These are in general the smaller plants that are harvested in whole or in groups. The individual plant is often at some stage used for food even though a number of plants are required for a meal. In some cases, as with lettuce and spinach, there are successive stages of gatherings, starting with thinnings and ending with good-sized plants. Plants usually treated thus include lettuce, radish, spinach, turnips, kohlrabi and mustard greens.

Two methods of broadcasting are useful. In either case, decide the area to be planted — often a wide band or series of bands across a garden mound — and how much seed to use. Then sprinkle the seeds by hand, swinging your arm first in one direction and then at right angles to try to have a uniform scatter pattern. You can also mix the seeds with a cup of dry soil or compost and spread the mixture. If the soil or compost is a contrasting color a visual indication of spread is provided. The second procedure works better for a beginner but with practice the first is satisfactory and a bit less trouble.

After the seed, which are all quite small, have been well distributed, they are raked in slightly and the whole area tamped lightly with a hoe.

Seed broadcast are ordinarily too small for you to put on much mulch before the plants are well up. If any mulch is applied, it should be needles or straw or lawn clippings and done lightly. The sides of the garden mound should be well mulched, however.

Speeding up germination is not needed for seed such as radish or lettuce, which germinate quickly enough if conditions are favorable. In other cases, however, additional steps are worthwhile in that they allow more efficient use of a small garden's space than simply seed storage before germination.

You may almost sprout overnight seeds of beans, peas, okra, corn, cucumbers, melons and squash by soaking them. If this is done, care may be necessary, especially with beans and peas, to see that the seed do not break apart. Of the above, okra is particularly notable for being a slow germinator so soaking may save a week or more germinating time.

Some seed have very special requirements for speeding up germination. In hot weather, for example, lettuce will germinate much better if refrigerated two or three days just prior to planting. Seeds of perennial herbs germinate very slowly but their dormancy can be broken by repeated freezing and thawing. Do this by placing these seeds alternately for an hour each in and out of the freezer over a period of a few hours.

Seeds of legumes should be inoculated with one of the commercially available bacterial preparations to increase the nitrogen-fixation that bacteria of the genus *Rhizobium* perform in nodules in their roots (see pp. 45-46).

A living mulch is a help for small seeds to germinate, especially if they do so slowly. For this purpose, sow radishes along with such small seed plants as lettuce, beets, carrots, kohlrabi, tomatoes, peppers, broccoli, parsley, okra and others. The quickly germinating radishes shade the ground and minimize any tendency for the soil to crust over. In addition, the shade decreases the likelihood of weed trouble and the radishes provide a quick bonus without decreasing the yield of the main crop.

Most seed germinate more quickly if the soil is lightly tamped just after planting. The reason is that closer contact is made between seed and soil particles and in this condition soil moisture reaches the seeds more efficiently by capillary movement. This is also a reason that a rather fine-grained soil or one with a high humus content induces more rapid germination than course sand.

Vines growing on a fence or on stakes naturally require less space than if allowed to sprawl. Cucumbers, tomatoes, running peas and beans, and muskmelons can be grown on fences to save space. For ease in picking, the best arrangement is to have such vines in a single line on one side of a mound rather than growing on pyramids or rectangular fences. The other side of the mound can be used for a low-growing plant such as cabbage, beets or Irish potatoes, or the mound can simply be a narrow one devoted to the one fence-supported crop.

In spite of the figures, there are no really good rules of thumb for deciding spacing. Experience seems to be the only basis for reaching most desirable plant densities, especially for larger plants. There are several reasons for this. One is that different varieties of a single vegetable will have different enough growth patterns that space just right for variety "A" may be insufficient for variety "B" and excessive for variety "C". Further, the same variety for various reasons will grow very large in one garden but be much smaller in another. In addition, if plants are allowed to sprawl over the mulch, they require much more space than if either tied to or climbing on stakes or fence.

Humus, if newly discovered, would be considered a miracle drug for our soils.
The Author

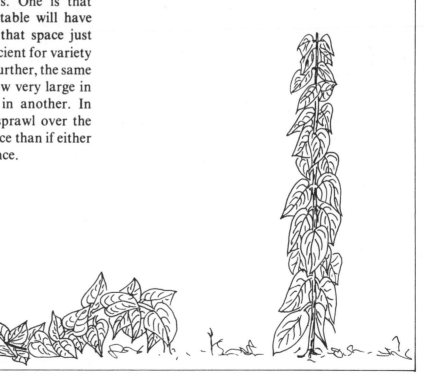

Staking avoids plant sprawl.

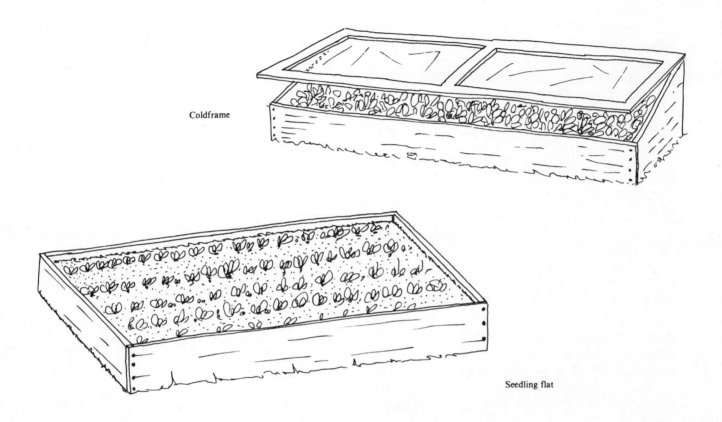

Coldframe

Seedling flat

Prestarting Plants.

Starting plants in greenhouse, coldframe, hotbed, or window sill can help make garden space go further, can provide an earlier start in the spring, or can increase the number of plants finally grown from a given number of seeds.

A useful method is to germinate seeds before planting them. Do this, if the number of seed used is very small, just as you would test to see if seed are viable. That is, roll the seed in moist absorbent paper (such as a paper towel) and place one end of the roll in water, using just enough water to keep the towel moist. Check daily and as the seeds germinate plant them in soil or compost in pots or paper cups or,

if the weather is suitable, outside in the garden. You may have better success this way with a number of plants than direct sowing in the garden. If larger amounts are needed, simply soak them overnight and then wash them gently each day to keep them moist. Plant the seeds at the first sign of sprouting or, in the case of beans or peas, when they have enlarged as much as they will. Soaking is especially useful for such slow-to-germinate seeds as okra, beets, chard, and parsley.

The more common prestarting method involves raising small plants for transplanting. (See p. 71). This practice is commonly used for tomatoes, peppers, eggplants, cabbage, broccoli,

collards, Brussels sprouts, and cauliflower and is increasingly being used for lettuce, melons, cucumbers and a few other food plants. There are several advantages in raising your own seedlings. You will have a much wider choice of varieties from seeds. There is less chance of introducing diseases. It is cheaper to raise your own plants, unless you want just a very few, and you will be less dependent on others. If you cooperate with one or more friends, the cost of seed becomes very low since most seed packets will be sufficient to raise transplants for several families.

Overwintering plants is an old story with perennials that are reasonably hardy, such as chives, mints, and many other herbs and flowers. In these cases, an extra thick layer of mulch will often keep the bulbs, roots or other parts viable, even though in many areas they come through the winters in good shape anyway. There is one precaution, however. Most of the mulch should be removed from immediately over the plants as soon as possible after regrowth starts in the spring. This may be six to eight weeks before the last expected frost in the case of chives and four to six weeks later for mints. Growth at that time is slow enough that being covered for an extra week or two probably makes little difference, so very frequent checks are not warranted.

Another possibility is overwintering of tomato, pepper, and herb plants in the house or in a greenhouse. Especially desirable plants may either be transferred to pots or cuttings can be rooted in the fall. Since this involves a vegetative process, the new plants (or the carry-overs) are genetically identical with the original and hybrids can be kept. It appears, too, that the carry-over plants may be more vigorous than new seedlings.

There is one precaution. If you succumb to the temptation to put out your over-wintered plants early, be sure to be prepared to take care of them through an unanticipated frost.

Certain plants are often found together in nature and others rarely, if ever, are associated. The most obvious reason is each plant has requirements which coincide or overlap or differ from those of another plant. In many cases the similarity or difference in requirements molds the distributions. In addition, however, the presence of one plant affects the growth or health of another. Companion planting takes advantage of this situation.

In other cases two or more plants may grow together with little or no interference. In such cases interplanting results in more efficient use of space with total productivity increased and sometimes with no decrease in any one crop.

Interplanting simulates nature with mixed stands of vegetables. One form of interplanting is discussed briefly here as companion planting. In the case of larger plants you may insert them individually or in small groupings. Thus you might have three or four small plantings of okra, three separate hills of cucumbers, two of muskmelons, etc., mixed in with lots of other plants.

Tables of companion plants and also some of the associations which certain writers on the subject recommend be avoided are given in several books on gardening (pp. 81-82), including Jeavan's *How to Grow More Vegetables,* Yepsen's *Organic Plant Protection,* and Mother Earth News' *Guide to Almost Foolproof Gardening.* Unfortunately, much of the literature is anecdotal and not based on controlled experiments. Some day there will be more carefully controlled experiments on both companion planting and interplanting so we will have a firmer basis for choices. The following comments point out some of the reasons why companion planting and interplanting are useful.

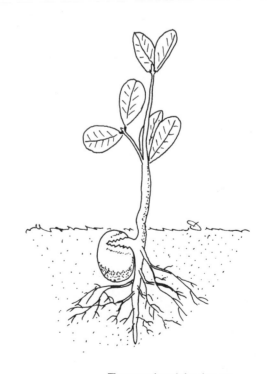

The pea seed cotyledon does not rise above the soil.

First, plants may occupy the same land but not the same airspace and the amount of shading either does no harm or is, in fact, beneficial. Squash or pumpkins growing among field corn provide a good illustration.

Plants may germinate and develop at quite different rates so that a rapid grower may provide favorable (or unfavorable) conditions for a slow growing plant. Radish and parsley are an excellent illustration, as is radish with lettuce or beets or carrots. Radish, lettuce and either tomatoes or okra provide a good three-tier succession when planted together. The radish shades and protects the surface for the less vigorous young lettuce and both protect the slower germinating and slow growing young tomato or okra. The yield of each is almost as great as if it alone occupied the space, providing quite a bonus.

The root systems of plants differ significantly in depth of growth; so adjacent or, preferably, intermixed plants using different depths of soil can serve as a basis for companion planting. Field corn interplanted with pumpkin or winter squash provides an example, the corn being the shallow-rooted partner. Additional combinations can be developed on the basis of information on page 71.

Corn and onion seedlings

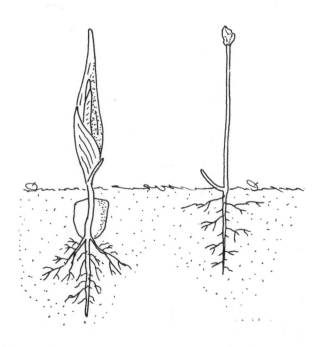

Plants having similar soil requirements may also be good combinations and those having quite differing requirements often do better separated. As an example, a soil very rich in nitrogen leads to excessive growth of leaves and stems and limited fruiting. Lettuce and other greens might flourish in such a soil while tomatoes would be a poor companion in this particular soil. Interestingly enough, plants appear to tolerate divergence from "normal" soil conditions better in humus-rich than in humus-poor soil.

Some plants are notable as insect repellants, presumably because of their odors. The onion family, parsley and other herbs, and marigolds are often interplanted with most any other plant as an insect deterrent.

The marigolds, which diminish the number of nematodes in the soil, are useful for this reason as well as others; and the edible Chinese chrysanthemums are said to perform the same nematode-control function. There are commercial marigold mixtures especially selected for nematode control.

Finally, a rich flora, as contrasted with a monoculture, is much less subject to devastating attacks of diseases or insects or other pests. For this reason, even without detailed knowledge of favorable combinations, the gardener who mixes the plants into a mosaic of individual plants or intermixes groups of plants will, on the average, realize a better yield from an area than would be obtained from large plantings of individual types. This is especially true if obvious space conflicts are avoided, based on one's experience. One application of this is to have rather widely scattered plants or groups of plants — a tomato plant here, another ten feet away, a third in the next garden; a small planting of beans one place, another fifty feet away; three cucumber plants, each in a different garden.

You will very likely have much less trouble with rabbits, insects and diseases among dispersed plants than among those growing in single-variety groups. It is certainly easier to interplant this way rather than to work out particular groupings. One apparent disadvantage is in picking. You have to go all over the gardens to pick tomatoes or okra or squash. This should be no problem, however, for the area is small and you can gather several different vegetables in one sweep around the garden.

Nurturing ...
The art of plant care

*... agriculture
ought to be as biologically
intensive and sophisticated
as we know how to make it.*
C.D. Freundenberger

CHAPTER SEVEN

There is much truth in the aphorism: Feed the soil and it will feed you. This is, however, only a part of a much broader principle: Maintain the health of the biosphere and it will support mankind.

There is a problem here, however. The biosphere — all life and its support systems —is too large for you personally to maintain though, left to its own devices, it has done an excellent job of renewing itself for hundreds of millions of years. On a smaller scale, however, an individual, family or community can do a great deal to aid in development of a healthy ecosystem with all the intricate relations of producers, herbivores, predators, parasites and decayers that find it to be their home. A garden placed in the midst of a dynamic, varied, and healthy ecosystem will have the advantages of all the checks and balances that provide for vigorous growth, usually with only tolerable losses to insects or diseases.

When conditions for good plant growth are maintained, plants are less likely to be seriously damaged if insects, bacteria or other organisms attack. The condition of the soil is one aspect of the garden that gardeners can do something about. Soil texture, soil moisture and air, various mineral nutrients, appropriate pH (for most vegetables about neutral or very slightly acid) and a good soil temperature are essential.

Information on cold tolerance is on page 70. In addition, however, there are two contrasting temperature needs. There is the need to let soil temperatures rise early in the spring so germination and growth can start and the need for keeping soil temperatures down in the heat of the summer so roots flourish and soil humus and nitrogen are preserved.

Best planting conditions are developed in late winter and early spring by over-winter mulching or growing a cover crop. The former has the advantage that no digging is needed prior to planting, so spring planting can often occur sooner than otherwise. The mulch has the advantage during winter that it keeps the soil somewhat warm as well as protected against winds. With the approach of spring, however, the mulch delays the normal rise in soil temperature. Brushing the mulch aside and exposing the soil surface directly to sunshine for several days raises the soil temperature several degrees so that planting can occur a week or two sooner than in still mulched areas.

During the growing season, however, high temperatures reached by exposed soil diminish root activity and so are unfavorable. At this time, a mulch is useful. Basically, there are three types of mulches available: non-decomposable, decomposable, and living mulches.

Avoid non-decomposable mulches such as plastic for several reasons. The most important is that while they protect the soil they do not nourish it. Because of this the soil will be a bit poorer each season that such mulches are used. In one study, production of strawberries was decidedly lower in plastic-mulched rows than when other mulches were used.

There is another non-decomposable mulch, however, that is useful in certain areas — rocks. In dry areas stones may be very important in water storage and so may be essential in non-irrigated gardens.

A much better mulch is made of decomposable materials such as leaves, hay, straw, lawn clippings, peanut hulls and so on, all of which during decomposition add humus and nutrients to the soil.

The third group of mulches is living plants which at least do not compete much with the crop being raised and may, in fact, complement it. For many smaller plants radishes are very useful companion plants, primarily because they serve as a living mulch. In the case of corn or okra, a low growing cover crop of soybean or even squash or pumpkins is a good companion for the same reason as well as for the additional production. Living mulches of legumes, because of the nitrogen fixation associated with them, are especially good for soil enrichment.

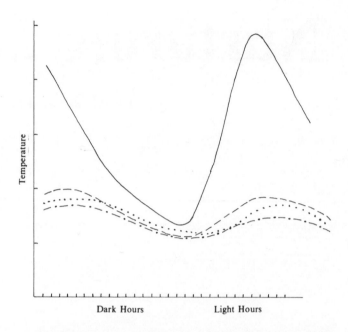

Generalized graph shows temperature fluctuations are greater in soil exposed to direct sunlight. The solid line shows typical variations in temperature of exposed soil on a summer day. Broken lines indicate temperature fluctuations with three mulches. *Which* mulch is less important than *whether* mulch is used.

Plants vary a great deal in how much soil moisture they require for optimum growth. Their roots have quite different distributions in the soil, also, as indicated in a table on page 71. In addition, soils differ greatly in moisture absorption, retention, and availability. As if there were not enough problems for farmer and gardener alike, water requirements are greatly affected by temperature, wind and humidity. In dry tropical areas, to grow some crops may require two or even three times the rainfall or irrigation necessary in moist, temperate climates.

On a long term basis the single most important solution to water problems is soil improvement.

Basically, the gardener has three approaches to meeting the water needs of plants. Often the simplest, easiest and cheapest way is to extend the usefulness of what rain does fall through mulching. Well mulched plants will often thrive through short rainless periods, such as two or even three weeks, with no evident ill effects. Coupled with the improvement in moisture relations of soil rich in humus, over some years a consistent mulching

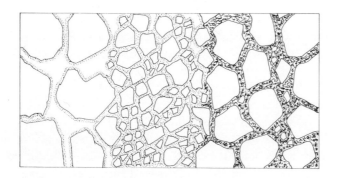

Particle size and organic content determine the water capacity of soil. Course sandy soil (left) with large spaces lets rain soak right through, leaving little moisture for plants. Loam with a mixture of particle sizes (center) or any soil with a combination of humus and inorganic particles (right) holds much larger amounts, making water and minerals more available to plants.

program can take care of the longer-term, second approach to the moisture problem — improving the soil's, capacity to retain and release water.

The third alternative is irrigation. Almost all gardeners will find there are times when irrigating is important. Two are especially notable. Light waterings are very useful for hastening germination of seeds and also after transplanting. Except for this, once a good soil has been built up — as the British would say, a soil of "good heart" — about the only time watering will be needed will be when there is an extended drought at a time of fruiting or rapid plant development.

The method of watering may in the long run be as important as whether you water or not. A light "once over" may do more harm than good for, unless the soil is moist to the level of deeper roots, the shallow roots of the plants will flourish and the deep ones not develop. Later, the rapid drying of surface layers will find plants unprepared for extracting the longer lasting and often more plentiful water deep in the soil.

Whenever the garden is watered, enough should be applied to either make contact with moist soil or to reach or go below the lowest root tips. It is a good practice to see how deep a certain amount of water will penetrate and on the basis of this calculate how much water should be applied at one time. One

way to do this is to measure the precipitation of a light rain or a sprinkling following a dry period and a day later dig down to see how far the water penetrated. For a good, loamy soil, an inch of rain should penetrate 15 or 16 inches after about half the available water has been used by the plants. Penetration will be deeper for sandy and less deep for clay soils.

How do you determine when to water? Probably the simplest way is to examine the soil under the mulch. A chart (p. 26) provides the necessary information on the appearance and feel of typical soils of differing textures. Another method is to observe the plants for possible wilting. If the plants droop somewhat at the end of a hot day, it is about time to water. If they are wilted early in the day, this is a sure sign the plant has suffered damage from dehydration because watering has been delayed too long. It is highly critical that plants not be stressed by water lack especially at times of rapid growth or development of edible parts. To illustrate, in the case of 20 square feet of snap beans, missing rain for a week or so before picking may cut the crop yield by half. For want of 20 or 30 gallons of water at a critical time, you may miss out on string beans for several meals.

There are many irrigating devices on the market. For sprinkling small beds or to water around transplants, nothing beats the oldfashioned watering can, especially the gentle-watering type that sprays the water upward so that it falls like a gentle shower.

Sprinklers are useful for irrigating a large area but much of the water evaporates before reaching plants or soil. In addition, water distribution is often poor.

For Survival Gardens with their long, narrow shape, probably the canvas soaker is the best of all. It is laid lengthwise of the garden right over the mulch and the water seeps in dropwise. A relatively inexpensive timing device can be attached at the spigot so that the water is automatically cut off after a set period.

For very small areas with plants which do best with very nearly constant watering, a can with several small holes near the bottom or an unglazed pot with no bottom hole can be useful. Sink it into the ground almost to the rim and plant lettuce, cabbage, melons or other especially desired plants around it. Add water every other day or so if the pot is down to half full.

Under emergency circumstances, it is entirely possible that the accepted and presently reliable sources of water for irrigation most gardeners have will not be working since electricity or gasoline for pumping may be missing. A pond, spring or cistern could make the difference between a good and productive garden and a failure.

Soil tests should be performed from time to time. A new garden requires testing annually and possibly seasonally but after three or four years less frequent testing will be adequate. These tests give information on soil pH and nitrogen, phosphorus and potassium available. Based on these tests, available resources can correct deficiencies. For a time, periodic additions of appropriate fertilizers should be made, rather than a single addition in the hope it will be effective forever. This is especially important with the inorganic, rapid-acting fertilizers. If these are used at all, try perhaps only ten percent of the recommended amount and repeat these small doses at intervals. If this is done, organic materials should continue to be applied also. They will interact with the quick-acting chemicals to extend the time of their availability and help offset the harmful effects of the salts in commercial fertilizers on the soil fauna and flora which are essential to maintenance of the best growing conditions.

For survival, you should not let yourself be "addicted" to commercial fertilizers which in emergencies may not be available. Remember, too, that their mining, manufacture, and transport require large amounts of energy and in some cases result in serious pollution problems. Using the leaves, manure and wastes available to many free or at little cost, it should be possible to develop and maintain most any soil for high production with little or no fertilizer purchases. A table on page 74, lists representative concentrations of nitrogen, phosphorus and potassium of a number of materials you may use for fertilizing your small garden. The associated discussion tells how to combine this information and fertilizer recommendations to determine appropriate soil additives to correct NPK deficiencies or imbalances.

You often hear that there is insufficiency of minerals in soils. This is probably seldom true as stated. The problem is not insufficient amounts of minerals but rather that too little is in an available form. Any amount of mineral in the clay, silt or sand components of soil is useless until it is transformed into minerals dissolved in the soil moisture. The processes for bringing about such solution are of immense importance to those of you who are developing gardens for survival foods. (As long as inorganic commercial fertilizers are depended on, they appear to be less important and are often neglected. Unfortunately, the processes themselves are greatly diminished when not used or when they are underused. The technics here recommended aim to keep these mechanisms working and vigorous.)

*There are only two ways to farm:
Add fossil fuels
to the process or
know what you are doing.*
Gary Snyder

A logical question is whether the so-called organic methods, which depend on natural processes augmented by human efforts, can possibly maintain the yields developed through modern methods with heavy emphasis on energy-intensive resources. Perhaps the final word is not in yet, but several recent studies comparing "conventional" and "organic" yields have been published. On the whole, these show "organic" farm yields do average somewhat below those of conventional farms, though not greatly so. With their lower costs, however, the organic farmers come through economically as well as their more conventional peers and they have a better cash flow situation.

There is, however, another important comparison to make: Are the fluctuations in productivity greater or less in the two methods? William Lockerety of the Northeast Solar Energy Center in Boston and his associates in a comparison of 26 matched pairs of organically and conventionally managed fields found much greater variations in yield in conventionally managed fields than in organic ones. It was true that the very highest yield was in a conventionally managed field.

On the other hand, the lowest yields were likewise in conventional farming. The authors conclude that when growing conditions were otherwise poor "yields from the organic fields came closer to or even exceeded those of the conventional fields." In fact, in the four-year study the lowest yield per acre in the organic fields was about six times greater than the lowest in the conventional fields. Year-in-and-year-out, the organic methods are more reliable in yield and hence for survival purposes are better even if we disregard the fact that in emergency situations fertilizers and pesticides may be unavailable or difficult to obtain.

Deficiencies of minerals in certain soils have been known for a long time. However, a garden enriched with a wide variety of decayable or decayed organic materials and with the pH adequately adjusted is likely to present no problem in this respect for three reasons.

First, many nutrients present in soil are more available for plant use in those soils rich in organic matter and adjusted to a pH proper for the plants being grown.

Second, most organic matter used for soil enrichment or for mulch has a variety of minerals as inherent components and, during decay, these are made available to plants.

Finally, various microorganisms and fungi growing in humus-rich soils mobilize minerals from soils.

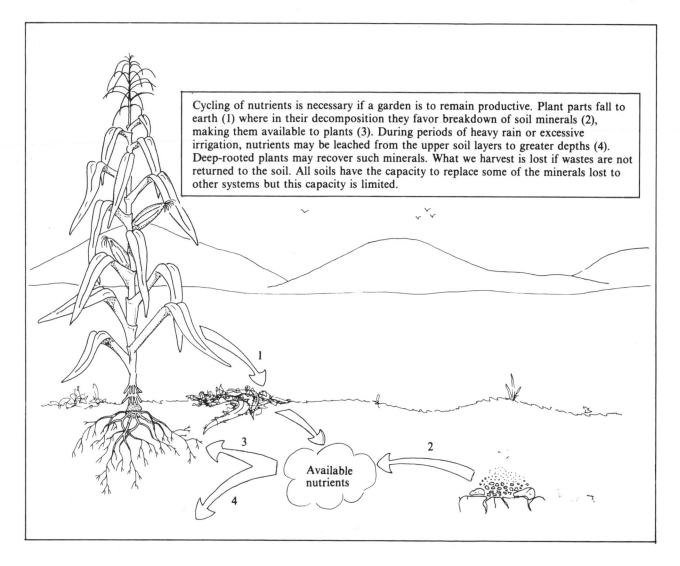

Cycling of nutrients is necessary if a garden is to remain productive. Plant parts fall to earth (1) where in their decomposition they favor breakdown of soil minerals (2), making them available to plants (3). During periods of heavy rain or excessive irrigation, nutrients may be leached from the upper soil layers to greater depths (4). Deep-rooted plants may recover such minerals. What we harvest is lost if wastes are not returned to the soil. All soils have the capacity to replace some of the minerals lost to other systems but this capacity is limited.

Available nutrients

The major nutrient that most often may be in low supply is available nitrogen, a deficiency indicated by poor growth with the leaves, especially lower ones, becoming pale green and finally yellow. Basically, you have two steps for overcoming nitrogen deficiencies in the Survival Garden. The most immediate and quick-acting is to provide a soil additive having a high content of nitrogen. These include various manures, blood, fish meal, horn and hoof meal, tankage and cotton seed meal. Nitrogen-rich mulches are slower acting but are especially useful for longer-term nitrogen enrichment. Such mulches include alfalfa hay or cuttings, most clovers, hairy vetch hay and hays of other legumes. Though it may not be available under emergency conditions, you may occasionally use very small amounts of a high nitrogen commercial fertilizer. Better yet, use some manure "tea" made by steeping manure in water and diluting the liquid to the color of weak tea.

The second method is to inoculate all legumes at planting and to include legumes as companion plants and in rotations. (See The Cheapest Nitrogen Fertilizer, pp. 45-46.)

One reason for development of a nitrogen deficiency is overcropping with non-leguminous plants. Another is over-use of low-nitrogen mulches such as insufficiently decayed sawdust or wood shavings or most straws and many hays. In the long run, these deficiencies can be remedied by interplanting peas, beans, soybeans and such legumes or by crop rotations that include the legumes each second or third year or by planting cover crops of legumes during fallow periods.

Loss of nitrogen may also be minimized by keeping the soil cool in hot weather and by growing organisms (whether plants or microogranisms) during fallow periods. In the former case, low soil temperatures decrease the rates of denitrification and also of breakdown of humus. Even the temperature lowering by a mulch is sufficient to bring about a significant saving of both fixed nitrogen and humus. The saving of nitrogen and also of other minerals by a cover crop or by microorganisms that use decaying materials results from their uptake of available minerals as they grow. Later as these organisms themselves decompose, the nutrients stored in them are released and so are made available to the plants you grow.

There are many other deficiencies but, to save space, it is suggested that you consult the table on mineral imbalances (pp. 76-77) and/or consult with your County Agricultural Agent or personnel of the Soil Conservation Service. In addition, it is a good idea to confer with these persons to see if there are specific mineral problems general in your area and what steps should be taken to remedy them.

Another feature for maintaining good growing conditions is to have the garden, if possible, set in a dynamic biological community with adjoining areas that provide food, nesting and reproductive areas, shelter and other needs of birds, toads, predatory insects and other organisms which can help maintain a balance of the various pests which are found in any garden.

In this respect, the best arrangement is either a forest edge north of the garden or other complex of plants or an imitation of such a natural system. The reason for this is that a complex biological community attracts and promotes the greatest variety of organisms. If there is space, then, you should ideally provide a mixture of trees, some adjoining shrubs and small plants and a bit of open water. Such a mix will meet the needs for shelter, nesting, food and water for a very complex assemblage of birds, insects, reptiles, amphibians and even some mammals. The result will be even more effective if several neighbors will cooperate in providing a larger area that is attractive for the desired predators.

Nesting boxes, safe watering areas, and winter shelters are also useful in keeping birds on duty throughout the year. In times when their natural foods are unavailable (especially during snow or ice storms), food should be provided for the birds.

Possibly as important is the maintaining of mulch under shrubs where the birds can work while protected from the wind and can find whatever seeds or other edibles remain. After a snow or ice storm, you will need to spruce up and to some extent replace much of the mulch because the birds have been so active.

An important feature of winter and early spring attraction of birds to the garden and its surroundings is that this is a time when pests will be at a minimum and the birds will reduce their numbers even more. Reduction at this particular time means the pest population starts the gardening season weakened and so is more easily controlled in the summer.

Should you develop a compost pile?

Those familiar with composting will readily recognize that the Survival Garden is a composting area as well as a food producer. Every mulched surface, whether on the planting bed, its slopes, or in the paths, is a site of intense breakdown of organic matter day and night. In my own gardens right now, in fact, about half a sack of leaves per square foot is composting each year, all our compostable kitchen wastes are being incorporated in the soil by burial, several trailer loads of mixed animal manures are used each year, and a fair quantity of wood ashes go in. With this active a composting schedule I do not feel a need for a separate structure called a compost pile. I do,

however, have a pile of woodchips that are decaying and will eventually be used as compost and another of sawdust and shavings with some manure that is used as a combination mulch/compost.

A compost pile is fine especially for limited space gardeners or for anyone who wants one, but I prefer to compost throughout my gardens.

Small Pond Good Sense

A small pond makes a great deal of sense as an adjunct to the Surival Garden. A pond can do several desirable things. Obviously it can provide a storage place for water and irrigation. Since some algae can fix nitrogen, a pond can be a fertilizer factory. Birds are attracted to water to drink. Toads, frogs and dragonflies spend early life in the water and all three serve in the insect patrol as adults. (Nymphs of the dragonfly also eat mosquito larvae.) Fish, frogs, crayfish and some aquatic snails are edible and so can augment the garden food supply. In fact, very small amounts of such foods can meet the requirement of vitamin B-12, a missing ingredient in most strictly vegetarian diets.

Size and location will be determined by perceived needs,

terrain and resources. If the idea is to provide breeding ground for toads and water for birds and nothing more, a half barrel or old bathtub sunk into the ground may do. If the pond is to provide incidental irrigation (a bucket of water now and then) a capacity of a hundred or more gallons is called for.

If you plan a concrete pond you will find directions available in how-to books on concrete and out-of-door construction in your library or pamphlets available from concrete outlets. If your ideas are more ambitious and you plan to dam a creek or develop a pond in a watershed having intermittent flow or have a dug pond where the water table is near the surface, you should consult the local Soil Conservation Service, Agricultural

Extension Agent or firms having experience in pond development.

There are two precautions. Even a small pond can be quite dangerous for a child and should be kept off limits to unattended children. Mosquitoes use ponds as breeding grounds. Many fish, however, will keep them under control. The small mosquitofish, native to much of the southern United States, is a very efficient mosquito eradicator, eating the larvae. They are winter hardy in areas where the water does not freeze all the way to the bottom. Goldfish can also be used to keep down mosquitoes but they will eat many tadpoles as well and so may defeat one of the purposes of having the pond in the first place.

Bees for Pollination

Plants we use for seeds or fruits or from which we save seed require pollination. In some cases, flower structure favors self-pollination, i.e., pollen from the stamen of a flower normally reaches the stigma of the same flower, as in peas. Some flowers (e.g., corn and other grains) are wind pollinated. Most garden vegetables are insect pollinated. Bees are often the effective transferrers of pollen from flower to flower and often a hive of bees can materially increase production. This is now especially true since the number of wild bees is much lower than in earlier days. There is not space here for details on bee keeping but an effective strategy is suggested and books listed in The Survival Gardener's Library (pp. 81-82) provide details.

When I decided several years ago to keep some bees, I had little idea of where to begin. My first step was to spend a couple of hours in the library reading issues of each of several bee journals. I chose one that suited my needs and subscribed to it. Six or eight months and several books later, I obtained two hive kits and ordered bees to be delivered in early April — some two or three months later. At the same time, I purchased a smoker, hive tool, bee veil and suit. Before the bees arrived I set up the hives after giving them three coats of a good housepaint.

When the two packages of bees came, I followed the instructions in introducing them to their new homes — except that in my initial excitement I forgot to smoke them. We got some honey that year but did not have enough buildup the second year for winter, so I had to start over again, poorer but knowing how to do better.

The care and maintenance of the bees and hive are well described in any of several introductory books on beekeeping, at least one of which should be thoroughly studied before the bees arrive. In my case, I now use two hive bodies per colony so that the bees can store plenty of honey for overwintering. Over these I place one or two shallow supers which we use for comb honey. I have not tried to maximize production thus far but have had an increase in production each year since restarting and feel I am improving in my hive management. We get plenty of honey for our own needs and last summer gave away as much as we saved. Since our purpose is to develop a degree of self-sufficiency and to have good pollination, this is enough.

The Cheapest Nitrogen Fertilizer

Among the plant nutrients, one stands out: it is most often in limited supply, and it can be lost from the soil by more routes than other nutrients. On the positive side, however, it is easily and cheaply "produced" right in place. This nutrient is nitrogen.

In nature, several nitrogen-fixing processes are known, i.e., several processes by which gaseous nitrogen of the atmosphere, which is not usable by most plants, is converted into a form which can be assimilated in plants and so indirectly made available for nutrition of man and other animals. While all of these nitrogen-fixing processes are important, we can do nothing about one but three can be aided by our efforts.

First, the one we can do nothing about. Lightning is notable for fixing nitrogen in the atmosphere. The nitrogen so fixed appears in all forms of precipitation and, of course, is widely distributed.

In the soil there are nitrogen fixing bacteria and fungi. Though widely distributed, their contribution to nitrogen fixation is limited to certain soil conditions. They require some organic food and can use many different ones. Some require a near neutral pH — about 7.0 is ideal but they tolerate down to about 6.5. And they require a soil not already too highly enriched with nitrogen. Several experiments show that the bacterium *Azotobacter* enhances plant growth but the reasons for this are not entirely clear. Certainly the nitrogen they fix is important but it appears they also improve the availability of other elements and secrete rootgrowth promoting materials. The Survival Garden that is well mulched appears ideal for *Azotobacter* provided that the pH is kept high enough.

The other processes are applied to gardening and agriculture. The next of these is little deliberately used in America but is much used in the Orient. Especially in rice paddies, in the Orient advantage is taken of the fact that certain algae (and also an aquatic fern, *Azolla*) can fix nitrogen. We could take advantage of this method of nitrogen fixation in Survival Gardening and at the same time improve our gardening and even food supply in the process. The only requirement is water in which algal growth is encouraged. The "pea soup" water is

Care for the soil; then sow the seed.
Sunithi Narayan

then used for irrigation, probably best by bucket or sprinkling can since the algae would quickly clog the pores in soakers or even the hole in sprinklers. The additional bonus from this nitrogen-fixing process is that the pond can be used to raise fish, crayfish or even snails which can be delicacies on the table or can be used for breeding toads to increase these valuable insect eaters. Either way, the whole effect is positive. Researchers at the Battelle Memorial Institute — Northwest have fertilized tomato plants with algae and obtained 45% more growth than when the same level of commercial nitrogen fertilizer was used. Such a substitution also saves a very considerable amount of energy as well as money.

A more widely used method of providing for nitrogen fixation takes advantage of bacteria of the genus *Rhizobium* which live symbiotically in the roots of many leguminous plants such as beans, peas, vetches, lespedezas, clovers, and soybeans. These bacteria carry out the process of nitrogen fixation, supplying the host plant with nitrogen in a useful form, and receiving their own non-nitrogenous nutrients from the host. Later when the roots and other remains of the plant decay, the nitrogen is added to the soil and the bacteria are dispersed where they may invade the next appropriate plant.

In the U.S., many soils already have appropriate strains of *Rhizobium* for beans, peas and some other legumes but most do not have the proper strain for some other legumes, notably soybeans — unless these have been grown recently in the soil and an inoculum was used at that time.

In view of the fact that commercially available strains of *Rhizobium* are highly efficient and generally more so than the organisms already in the soil and the bacteria may not survive from year to year in sufficient numbers for maximum effect, inoculation of all legume seeds each time they are planted is worthwhile.

However, since disruptions of the inoculum industry or distribution can occur in the future, each type of legume should be grown in various parts of the garden. At least there is a chance that in a subsequent year enough organisms will be present to naturally inoculate any legume seed planted.

When the plants die, let them decay in place and so disseminate the desired bacteria pretty much throughout the various garden mounds.

To make sure the inoculation was successful, dig up one or two of each type of mature plant, wash off the soil adhering to the roots, and check for knotty growths, called nodules, on the roots, especially on the largest roots at the base of the plant. If nodules are found, cut into or crush a few of them. If they are reddish, brown or green, the *Rhizobium* has set up housekeeping and you are in business. (The red nodules are currently active; brown and green ones have been active and so indicate successful inoculation.) White or gray colors indicate the bacteria are not suited to the particular legume. These are probably from wild and in this combination, at least, ineffective strains of the bacteria. If these are found, the next crop should certainly again be inoculated.

After a garden has thus been thoroughly inoculated, subsequent plantings in a rotation may develop nodules without further use of the purchased inoculum and possibly as much as a hundred pounds or even more free nitrogen fertilizer is provided each year for each acre planted in legumes. That is cheap and easily applied fertilizer independent of energy-intensive commercial nitrogen fixation. However, in view of the possibility of too few remaining viable until the next planting, as long as inocula are readily available, they should be used at each planting — for cheap insurance.

There are some precautions that need emphasis. Perhaps the foremost is that any one bacterial strain is effective with only a limited range of legumes. One species, *R. phaseoli,* for example, is effective with string beans, navy and kidney beans. *R. leguminosarum* is active in peas. Yet another species colonizes lima beans. Since the above types

of bacteria are often found in soil, inoculation may not increase the nitrogen-enriching capacity when these legumes are grown. The bacterium for soybeans, *R. japonicum,* has only recently been widely introduced into American soils so chances are high that a particular garden may not have sufficient bacteria to realize the full benefit of growing soybeans.

Most seed treatments intended for decreasing seed destruction by bacteria and molds during germination will either kill or inhibit the nitrogen-fixing bacteria. If you are not certain that your seeds are untreated it is safest to plant the seeds and, after they germinate, inoculate the area by sprinkling the emerging plants with water in which the appropriate bacteria have been well dispersed. Another possibility is to use the granular *Rhizobium* preparations that are placed in the furrow or on the ground at the time of planting.

The soil pH and organic matter content also affect the symbiotic nitrogen fixers. A soil rich in organic matter and at a pH of about 6.5 to 7.0 appears ideal for these organisms, so in areas where the soil is more acid than pH 6.5 wood ashes, agricultural lime, or dolomite should be applied, preferably ahead of planting time, to adjust the pH to the recommended range.

One final precaution. Leguminous plants "produce" some nitrogen if grown for brief periods but for maximum effect most must be grown for a long time. Recent reports from Canada and Michigan indicate that at least one strain of the English broadbean fixes nitrogen in a much shorter season than most legumes -- in as short as six weeks.

In nature nothing is wasted, for everything is part of a continuous cycle.
Dennis Hayes

Diseases and Pests ...
Some natural controls

*The preventive
operations are those
of the best culture ...
If these are carefully
attended to, it will
seldom happen that
any species of insect
will exist in the garden
to an injurious degree.*
Encyclopedia of Gardening, 1824

CHAPTER EIGHT

Control for diseases and pests is currently one of the most controversial aspects of gardening and farming. Great emphasis has been placed on use of a wide variety of chemicals. In recent years, however, there has been in the United States and elsewhere a growing movement, especially among gardeners but increasingly among farmers as well, to use "organic", biological and integrated methods of pest and disease control. A most favorable development is integrated pest management (IPM) which applies a variety of technics with emphasis on cultural and biological controls backed by chemical pesticides in the case of an outbreak. Carefully applied and with good, knowledgeable management, this combination in commercial farming often costs less, uses less labor in some cases, and decreases the amounts of poisons used.

In some respects the small-scale gardener has the same problems with respect to pests as the large-scale farmer — or, at least, so it would seem. In fact, however, and for all practical purposes, the small-scale gardener does not *have* to have these problems to a serious degree and the steps presented briefly below should diminish greatly or almost eliminate disease and pest problems.

The most basic ecological principle applied to pest control is that organisms have specific requirements for life and if these are not met the organism dies or does not thrive. Survival Gardening attempts to provide the conditions essential for those organisms desired, whether vegetables, fruits, flowers or predators, and at the same time to avoid the conditions favoring crop pests and disease producers. In addition, Survival Gardening uses methods to establish conditions specifically unfavorable to pathogens and pests.

These principles, especially if resistant plants are used, greatly decrease disease and pest problems.

Plant diseases usually refer to conditions caused by bacteria, viruses or fungi. If the particular pathogen is present, susceptible plants may be diseased.

Fortunately, most infectious organisms parasitize only one or a few closely related species so even if one type of plant can not be grown because of a disease this is no reason others will not thrive. If a particular disease is known to be present in an area, one preventive is to either avoid crops susceptible to the disease or to plant varieties that are not susceptible or are, to some extent, resistant. Most seed catalogs include information about disease resistance of the varieties listed and local farm seed supply sources and Agricultural Extension Agents have information on the matter.

You do not, however, have to limit your garden to resistant strains. Take advantage of the antibiotic properties of good soil assemblages to diminish the numbers of pathogens in garden soil and either crop rotation or interplanting — especially crop rotation — to reduce disease problems. The basic reasons are that organisms that lack a host generally have rather short life expectancies. And in rich soil there are many varieties of organisms, some of which through chemical or other means restrict the growth of many other organisms, especially microbes, just as penicillin and aureomycin do for some human pathogens. A regular program of soil enrichment favors development of a soil in which many nonparasitic organisms grow.

One factor in disease spread is insect vectors (carriers). Some diseases can be minimized by careful attention to insect control. Since many fungal diseases are easily spread when plants are wet, it is best to avoid handling wet plants. Tomatoes and peppers can be infected with tobacco mosaic virus so one should not use tobacco in any form in the garden.

If you are unfortunate enough to have your plants become infected, the usual best bet is to remove and burn the affected plant and then be sure not to plant the same type in that particular area for at least another two years, preferably longer.

You may use two general methods for introducing parasites and predators to help control insects. One is to have small gardens dispersed with a mixture of wild plants growing rather close on at least one side or end of each garden. Many predators, including insects, spiders, birds, lizards, toads and others, can get right in among your plants. The mulch is quite attractive as a feeding area for some birds in winter and in the summer provides a hiding place for toads. To supplement these "natives", introduce ladybugs, praying mantis, ichneumon wasps and other predatory insects which can be purchased by mail from a number of sources.

However, unless conditions favoring the introduced predators are maintained the effect of introduction will be short. It logically follows that creating conditions in and around the garden favorable to desired predators is essential for this tactic to be successful. Since the predators are likely to be present in small numbers anyway, it is wise to use this step rather than introducing foreign predators; or if predators are introduced, to first create garden conditions favoring them. The easiest way to do this is to maintain a high diversity of plants (cultivated and/or wild) in and near the garden. Both known and unrecognized predators in great variety will be present at all times, ready to act quickly if pests start to get out of hand at the very same time that the diversified flora minimizes the chance any pest will become a problem.

You may purchase disease organisms against certain insects. The cole plants (cabbage, broccoli and relatives) and some other plants are often attacked by cabbage worms. A most effective control for these is a bacterium, *Bacillus thuringiensis,* preparations of which are available under several trade names. This is also effective against the tomato hornworm, cornworms and a number of other pests.

Also deliberately spread is milky spore disease which attacks Japanese beetles in the larval stage and quite a number of similar but frequently less serious pests. The milky spore disease organism also comes under several trade names. One is a white powder which is dropped in teaspoon-size doses over grassy areas.

The commercially available predators and pathogens are all easily applied in the small garden, inexpensive and quite effective. Undoubtedly more will become available in the years ahead so keep an eye out for them, just in case. This method of pest control will become increasingly important as our awareness of problems created by persistent chemicals increases and the cheap energy of yesterday loses its lingering effects on us.

Incidentally, biological controls are most effective if applied over considerable areas since insects from surrounding infested areas easily move onto the small property. For this reason, it would be most helpful if whole communities or at least neighboring gardeners would coordinate their insect control programs.

A few pests deserve individual mention as you will find on pages 51-53. Persons having other insect problems would do well to consult their local Agricultural Extension Agents for advice on control or to refer to books dealing with integrated or "organic" pest control technics. (See The Survival Gardener's Library, pp. 81-82.)

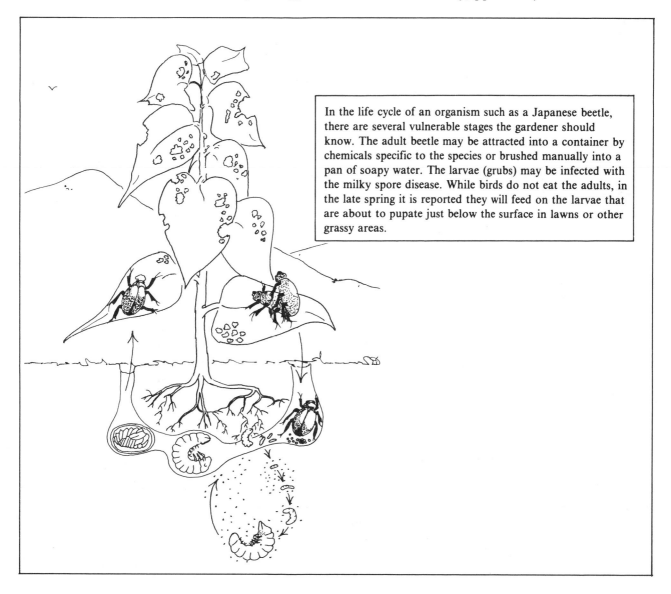

In the life cycle of an organism such as a Japanese beetle, there are several vulnerable stages the gardener should know. The adult beetle may be attracted into a container by chemicals specific to the species or brushed manually into a pan of soapy water. The larvae (grubs) may be infected with the milky spore disease. While birds do not eat the adults, in the late spring it is reported they will feed on the larvae that are about to pupate just below the surface in lawns or other grassy areas.

Six Helpful Insects

Lacewing (2x)

Preying mantis (1x)

Lady bug (4x)

Syrphid fly (3x)

Ichneumon wasp (1x)

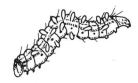

Braconid wasp
Coccoons on caterpillar (1x)

I have been fortunate in having little problem with disease in my garden these last few years but before that I had considerable experience with insects in great variety and large numbers. Few of my crops have ever been complete failures but I have had my share of disasters. My experience in recent years, however, has been very different.

I find two things help more than anything else to reduce insect damage in gardens: cultural practices which bring together a mixture of plant types and introducing or coaxing control organisms into the gardens. In Africa and Europe I observed non-monoculture vegetable gardens — plants of various types deliberately being grown together to imitate the situation most frequent in nature. It appears that insects can not as readily find new plant hosts to attack under these circumstances and it is entirely possible the chemical senses by which they locate new plants for feeding or egg laying do not function as well when certain types are interplanted.

There are some important varietal differences in susceptibility to insect damage. The most notable is the high resistance of the butternut squash, a fine winter variety, to the squash vine borer. Another, the various types of corn forming very tight shucks around the ears are less likely to have corn borer damage than those with loosely fitted shucks.

One study, conducted at Cornell University some years ago, showed a distinctly lower incidence of insect damage to collards when the plants were separated from each other by tomatoes. Herbs are often planted among vegetables because they appear to repel certain insects.

*Pest control is
basically an ecological,
not a chemical problem.*
Robert L. Rudd

Aphids

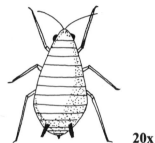

20x

Two aphid controls that are
often sufficient are growing garlic
around especially susceptible plants
in a permanent location, such as
shrubs, and using ladybugs. At
times water squirted on plants will
foil the aphids. They should
usually present little problem where
a mixture of plants are grown
together. In areas where aphids are
especially bothersome, interplanting especially susceptible
plants with garlic, chives or other
onions is often highly effective for
long-term control while a spray of
nicotine sulfate may be used for
quick results.

Cutworms

1x

Cutworms are insect larvae
that chew through many plants
mostly early in the growing season.
They are more of a problem in
newly established gardens.

Cutworms are favored foods
of toads and birds so if these are
attracted to a garden control may
be almost complete. A control
method adapted to transplants is
wrapping the stem with a
cardboard or paper collar

extending about an inch below and
two inches above the soil surface at
the time of transplanting or
sticking two or three small sticks
into the ground right against the
stem of the transplant.

Flea beetles

These are small beetles, often
of dark color or striped, about a
sixteenth inch long that attack
many plants, especially young ones.
They may attack a few days after
transplanting and if not controlled
kill the young plants very quickly.
A very effective control is to dust
rather heavily with rotenone
powder and to repeat this
treatment if the beetles reappear.
One to three treatments are usually
sufficient. You may have to repeat
occasionally on a mature plant.
Another control that appears to
work is to dust the young plants
with wood ashes every two or three
days.

Japanese beetles

Japanese beetles (see p. 49)
are a serious problem,
actually best attacked on a
community-wide basis.

Mexican bean beetle

4x

The Mexican bean beetle is
often a major pest. Its oval shape,
quarter inch length, copper or
brownish color and spots are
distinctive. It is more likely to be a
problem late in the bean season.
Hand picking and destroying not
only the adults but the yellowish or
orange larvae and egg clusters is
practical in small scale gardening if
consistently practiced from the
earliest signs of the bean beetle.
Praying mantises are effective
beetle predators since they can
work all over the host plant.
Interplanting beans with potatoes,
nasturtiums or garlic is said to
diminish Mexican bean beetle
attacks and would be especially
suited to small gardens.

Grasshoppers

1x

Every competent gardener becomes an ecologist.

The Author

Effective control may be by steps to foster birds, lizards, toads, spiders, and such by having a mixture of wild plants, perhaps in fencerows. Though weedy areas and fencerows are favorite breeding grounds for grasshoppers, their fostering of predators more than counterbalances this effect. Praying mantis, chickens and guineas are also efficient grasshopper predators.

Blister beetles

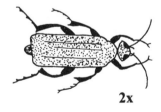

2x

These are obnoxious insects about a half inch long, black with white stripes lengthwise, with a slightly swollen abdomen. Left alone, they can completely destroy affected plants. A mixed garden within a vigorous and diversified ecosystem appears to be the best preventive for their attacks. If some do appear, brushing them into a jar of soapy water is effective if used early in an attack.

Squash vine borer

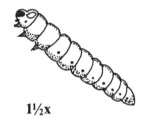

1½x

The adults lay eggs on the squash vine and the newly hatched larvae invade the stem or, late in the season, the fruit. Their presence can be told by exudates from small holes in the squash vines or fruit. Several control technics are possible. Derris root or sabadilla dust powders may be sprinkled on the stems starting at an early stage and continuing at weekly intervals. Some persons have found progressive covering of the stems helpful. In a small planting, slitting the stems lengthwise at the affected areas and removing the worms can be effective. Another recommended control method is "mulching" under squash (perhaps *over* a regular leafy mulch) with aluminum foil.

Hornworms

These are dramatic pests because of their large size and at times complete defoliation of attacked plants. It may be recognized by a horn-shaped protrusion near the rear of the body. Some varieties grow to two or three inches while others may grow even larger. The hornworms attack a number of plants, especially tomatoes and dill. Dill, in fact, is sometimes used as a trap plant, since the worms are especially easy to see on it. Hand picking can be an effective control since hornworms are usually found in small numbers.

2/3x

There is one precaution, however. The hornworm is often attacked by a parasitic braconid wasp which lays its egg in the hornworm. After hatching, the young braconids feast on their host and finally form white pupae which project from the worm's surface. If these pupae are found, the hornworm should not be disturbed. Its days are numbered and the wasps will soon be off to attack again. In case of a serious problem with the hornworm, *Bacillus thuringiensis* can be used against them with good, rapid results as a short term measure.

Colorado potato beetle

4x

These are well-known insects yellow to white with brown or black stripes, about a half-inch long, that are especially likely to attach potatoes, eggplants, tomatoes and peppers. When an invasion is starting, especially, hand picking of the adults, eggs (usually found on the undersides of leaves), or reddish larvae is an effective control. Interplanting with beans or marigolds is often recommended and the beetles seem much less a problem in gardens where many plants are grown mixed together.

Only the whole big system works.
T.T. Thomas

Nematodes

The nematodes or round worms are a universally distributed group of parasites for plants and animals. Fortunately, any one nematode species can invade only one or a few hosts. In fact, if we knew enough we could identify most plants and animals by studying the nematodes on or in them.

A number of experiments, including quite carefully controlled ones, have shown that nematode damage in some plants can be significantly reduced by cultural means. One of the most specific controls is interplanting with French and African marigolds. These should be grown to maturity and finally incorporated into the soil for greatest efficiency. Seed companies have a special mix of marigolds suited to this purpose.

Crop rotation is also useful in nematode control. Perhaps the single most general and inexpensive method is to increase the soil fungal population by incorporating organic matter in the soil.

Chinese chrysanthemums are said to affect nematodes as do marigolds, and they are also edible.

Rabbits.

Rabbits are a pest in most gardens. Seldom are there now a sufficient number of natural predators to keep them in check. A dog or perhaps even a cat is a help but many gardeners will find more help is needed. The greatest damage from rabbits occurs when they have many plants of the same type together to feast on. A single rabbit in a night may ruin a nice row of beans or young cabbages. When plants are mixed together, however, there is usually much less

damage. If you have twenty broccoli plants scattered through the gardens, for example, a rabbit is much more likely to take one or two and miss the others. In a row, many more would be taken. Wire fencing about 30 inches wide placed around individual plants or small plantings is a more sure control.

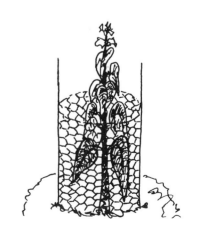

Herbs and Other Plants Reputed to Repel Pests

Pest	Reputed repellant
Ants	English pennyroyal, spearmint, southernwood, tansy, nasturtium
Aphids	Ant repellants (above), garlic, onions chives, garlic chives, coriander, anise, nasturtium, petunia
Cabbage worm	Mint, tomato, rosemary, sage, peppermint, hyssop, southernwood, thyme, wormwood, catnip, nasturtium
Carrot fly	Rosemary, sage, wormwood, garlic, onions, chives, coriander
Colorado potato beetle	Green beans, horseradish
Cucumber beetle	Tansy, radish
Cutworm	Tansy
Fleabeetle	Wormwood, mint, catnip
Flies	Basil, tansy
Japanese beetle	Garlic, tansy, rue, larkspur
Leafhopper	Petunia, geranium
Mexican bean beetle	Marigold, potato, rosemary, summer savory, petunia
Mice	Mint
Mites	Garlic, chives, garlic chives, onions
Mosquitoes	Basil, tansy
Nematode	African and French marigold, pot marigold, scarlet sage, Chinese chrysanthemum
Rabbit	Garlic, onion, chives
Snails, slugs	Prostrate rosemary, wormwood
Squash bug	Tansy, nasturtium, radish
Tomato hookworm	Borage, pot marigold, opal basil
White fly	Nasturtium, marigold, Peruvian ground cherry
Wireworm	White mustard, buckwheat, woad

I suspect that the insects which have harrassed you have been encouraged by the feebleness of your plants; and that has been produced by the lean state of your soil.

T. Jefferson

Harvesting ...
The work and the joy of it

*The most important event
on Earth each year
is the harvest.*
Robert C. Tetro

CHAPTER NINE

Harvest time may be the happiest of all gardening seasons. The results of your labor and planning show and you discover that gardening in natural cycles does work.

You will learn to recognize when your own vegetables are nearly like those in the better markets but you will need to notice a number of beginning signs and to start noticing varietal differences in maturity.

Size is the primary cue in a number of cases, including radishes, turnips, rutabaga, beets, summer squash, cucumbers, okra, carrots, eggplant, onions, peppers, and chard. All of these are edible smaller than usually picked, but they often are poor quality when they are allowed to grow too long. If unacquainted with a new variety, start picking it early and then try larger ones. You will soon find the best sizes for your own conditions. As an example, you may pick yellow straightneck squash from three to fifteen inches long and find it great for some uses at 3 or 4 inches, for others 5 or 6, but find the quality drops sharply as the fruits grow larger than this. With okra the magic figure is two to four inches. Just what variety one is growing, however, is a critical factor in picking size. One variety of cucumber may be just right at 4 or 5 inches; another may be just as good at 8 or even 10. Many vegetables usually considered simply for cooking are delicious eaten raw if picked early.

Leafy plants give a good chance for creative picking. Early on, combine thinning and harvesting of lettuce, mustard, turnip greens, spinach and chard. Later harvest only the outer leaves for a while and finally take the whole plant. Beets and onions and on occasion thickly planted cabbages can be treated this way.

Beans and peas present special challenges to the harvester. All can be allowed to mature and be used dried. On the other hand, most gardeners want the immature seeds or pods for the table. In the case of butterbeans and peas that are shelled (the hulls are not eaten) the pod thickens before they are ready for picking. If you are inexperienced, watch to see when the pods show a series of swellings and open one or two. If these are too small, leave the others to swell some more. Experience is the only reliable teacher in this case.

Edible podded beans and peas (snap beans, snowpeas, sugar snaps) come in two general types. In some, the seeds themselves are either not yet enlarged or the enlargement is not apparent unless the pod is opened. In these cases size is at first the most reliable guide to proper maturity. As you find some are fibrous you will realize there are other more subtle indicators and will come to use these as well. However, sugarsnaps and some snap beans show definite signs of seed enlargement beforehand. Once this thickening has occurred, picking should not be delayed.

With string beans you will find the best picking size will vary not only from variety to variety but all through the season. Early in the season the beans seem best at the smallest sizes but later, especially in the fall, rather large beans can be very good. Summer or fall, however, when the beans are allowed to overgrow, the shelled beans, whether green or dry, are delicious. Likewise, older butterbeans should not be discarded but may be used in soups or stews or even used right along with the green ones.

In the case of broccoli, you will want to pick it when the buds have enlarged but the flowers have not opened. There will be one or a few days for any one floret to be in just this condition. Right then cut off the stem below the cluster far enough back that the stem is tough — perhaps a foot back. This way you are not only harvesting but pruning at the same time. If the variety is one which sends out secondary florets, leave the base of the plant alone. If it is a "one-shot" plant, pull it up and make room for something else.

Irish potatoes are dug when the plants start dying or are dead. Most gardeners, however, relish some early potatoes and feel under the mulch to find them about the time an occasional flower appears. If your soil is very well developed, you may grapple in the hill with your hand and quickly locate almost all the potatoes. In a small planting, this is a pleasant job and it has the distinct advantage of not damaging the potatoes themselves.

Winter squash and pimento and paprika peppers for grinding and to some extent some melons are diagnosed as mature by color. Descriptions of winter squash and muskmelon will indicate their appearances at picking. In addition, the muskmelon may have a fruity odor when ready and the fruit will loosen from the stem easily. Pimento and paprika peppers will be a brilliant and uniform red at maturity. (Incidentally, pimentoes picked while green can be used just like bell peppers and paprika peppers are delicious when fried green.)

Corn presents a special problem. It is best when the grains have enlarged and the milky contents flow out when broken. Browning of the silks provides a cue but most inexperienced corn gatherers will need to open the husk a bit and mash a grain with the thumbnail. If the grains are hard or show signs of shrinking, the corn is too mature for roasting ears or fresh corn but it can be used in soups and stews.

It is more important to pick vegetables at the right time than to have enough for a meal. After all, many bits and pieces can be put into soup or salad and add as much nutrition there as they would in a larger serving of a single vegetable.

For an excellent article on picking vegetables, see one by Ray Wolf, "Picking Vegetables at Perfection" (Organic Gardening, July 1979, pp. 48-54).

Preserving your produce is a topic in itself. You will want to study this carefully. Carol Stover's book, *Stocking Up,* provides as complete a discussion of this as you will find anywhere.

Something else you will want to harvest and preserve is your own seeds from this year's gardening efforts for next year's Survival Garden.

Typical Times to Maturity, Lengths of Harvest		
Vegetable	Time to maturity (weeks)	Length of harvest (weeks)
Bean, bush	7-9	2
Bean, pole	7-10	3
Beet	8-10	4
Broccoli	9-11	6
Brussels sprouts	17-22	3
Cabbage, common	7-14	6
Cabbage, Chinese	6-8	4
Carrot	10-11	3
Cauliflower	9-13	2
Chard	8-13	Until frost
Collard	6-10	9
Corn	11-14	1-2
Cucumber	8-9	4
Eggplant	8-11	Until frost
Kale	7-10	9
Kohlrabi	7-9	2
Lettuce	7-12	3
Muskmelon	12-13	4
Mustard	6-7	4
Okra	8-9	Until frost
Onion, spring	13-17	6
Parsnip	17	—
Parsley	11-12	Until frost
Peas	9-17	1-2
Pepper	9-11	Until frost
Potato	10-13	—
Radish	3-4	1-2
Rutabaga	10-14	4
Salsify	4-7	—
Soybeans	10-18	1-3
Spinach	6-8	3-4
Squash, bush	7-8	5-6
Squash, vine	12-14	5-6
Sweetpotato	13-21	—
Tomato	9-12	Variable; some varieties until fall frost.
Turnip	6-9	4

While the earth remainest, seedtime and harvest ... shall not cease.
Genesis

... the scientists have not yet explored the hidden possibilities of the innumerable seeds, leaves and fruits for giving the fullest possible nutrition to mankind.
Mohandas Gandhi

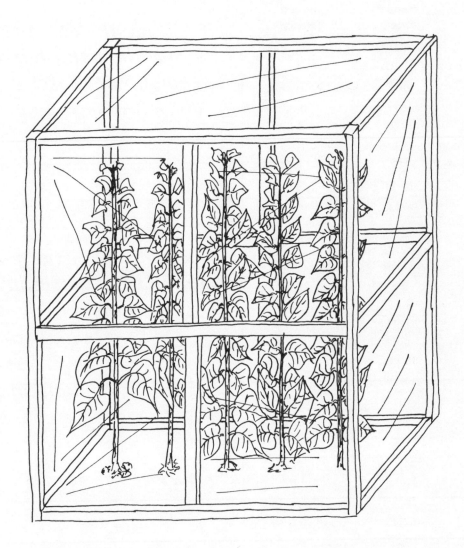

Wind or insect pollinated plants must be isolated in cages or simply by distance from others with which they may cross. A screen wire or cheesecloth covering on a light frame such as is pictured here is often sufficient for insect pollinated plants. A close-meshed cloth can help prevent stray pollen blown by the wind from reaching enclosed plants.

Seedsman ...
You can be your own

The ability to save seed is ... one of the most valuable tools for self-sufficiency.
Kent Whealy

CHAPTER TEN

No garden is truly independent of outside human input unless some means of perpetuating the breeding stock of plants is used. If the situation for which we are preparing is a depression or high inflation, this may be a problem of no great consequence. On the other hand, should there be a large scale breakdown of the transportation and communications systems for any reason, your gardening could depend on your having seed stock and knowing how to maintain it.

Another situation in which local maintenance of seed stocks is important is the increasing constriction of food crop gene pools. That is, it is a practice in commercial gardening to use a much smaller number of varieties than at one time and the result is greater vulnerability to gene-related problems, as was shown in the loss of corn from a widespread blight a decade ago and in the potato famine of Ireland last century. If a large number of small gene pools is maintained, any genetically influenced disorder, such as various fungal, viral and bacterial infections, will be limited in its effects.

An ideal condition would be cooperative efforts to develop and maintain strains of vegetables and fruits adapted to local climate and soil. In this way several individuals in the community would preserve the genetic pool of a desired plant while others would similarly specialize in keeping others. Pending such a development, each gardener should develop the various skills required for stock maintenance. In this section the methods needed will be considered.

Very few gardeners today know in detail how to save their own vegetable seed, though this was common knowledge only three or four generations ago. Recovering a lost art such as this takes time.

Maintenance of breeding stocks for home gardens is potentially critical enough that some kind of fail-safe plan is called for. Such a plan is discussed briefly here.

The first step is to develop a list, including varietal names, of vegetable stocks to be maintained. It should include most of the Very Special Survival Vegetables plus a few others. It should certainly include a couple of legumes to help maintain soil, three or more of the high calorie producers, and some easily overwintered vegetables.

Next, obtain a two or more years' supply of each type of seed (except for the two types of potatoes, which are reproduced vegetatively).

Practice raising and collecting and storing your own seed and potatoes using commercial sources as backup until you have adequate reserves.

Each winter or very early spring run viability tests on your older stocks by keeping a few seeds moist in several layers of absorbent paper or cloth to see if they sprout. If as few as half of the seed sprout or if germination is slower than normal for the type, replace them.

As you find varieties better suited to your needs — as demonstrated in your own garden — phase out older varieties and replace them with the better ones.

The very simplest gene pool maintenance ordinarily occurs with no human intervention except taking certain precautions. Perennials — which includes shrubs, trees and many of our herbs — maintain themselves from year to year, usually with no particular attention. There are, however, two precautions. First, the stock should be large enough that a loss of one or two plants is immaterial. With herbs, for example, you may lose a few plants each winter. With several plants scattered so a single event does not affect all, you are unlikely to lose your stock. Share with friends and you will have a ready source for restarting if you lose a variety. The second precaution is to mulch perennial herbs, especially the least hardy ones, at about the time of the first frost. Combined with care in uncovering them in the spring, this enhances chances of survival.

As mentioned elsewhere, some annuals may be treated as perennials by potting them (or by rooting cuttings) and keeping them indoors in the winter. This is most feasible with tomatoes, peppers, herbs and such plants when only a few are needed. This method also has the advantage that desirable hybrids may be kept going.

Several herbs which are annuals or biennials are in a category by themselves — they will reseed themselves. The major work involved in maintaining the stock is keeping growing conditions good, recognizing the seedlings and protecting them each spring and avoiding varietal cross pollination by keeping only a single type. Dill, fennel and basil are annuals and parsley, a biennial, that in many areas will self seed. Anyone who wants to keep two or more varieties of any of these will have to take steps to prevent cross pollination. This may be as simple as keeping variety "A" clipped so it doesn't flower for a couple of weeks while variety "B" flowers and then reversing the process. Other possibilities will be apparent from the following discussion.

Plants which are vegetatively reproduced constitute a special group. There are plants whose seeds generally are not used for reproducing. This includes strawberries of most types, Irish potatoes, sweetpotatoes, Jerusalem artichoke, some onions, chives and garlic. Except for sweetpotatoes, in many areas these can all be saved right in the ground with some protective mulch. Where winters are too cold or mice or other pests may destroy the overwintering parts, the reproductive structures must be stored over the winter at a low but not freezing temperature.

Some plants self pollinate exclusively or to such a high degree that no particular precautions against cross pollination, other than perhaps a few feet separation between varieties, is required. Peas, beans, okra and tomatoes are therefore very simply managed. To save seed from the first three is especially easy: select the best plants and allow the pods of these plants to mature. When the pods are thoroughly dry, separate the seeds. In the case of tomatoes, select the best fruit on the finest plants and allow them to mature thoroughly. Pick the tomatoes, scoop out the seed with as little pulp as practical and place in a jar with water to cover the pulp and seeds. Allow the material to ferment until most of the seeds separate and lie on the bottom. Rinse the seeds well to remove remaining pulp, spread them out, and dry them in the shade.

The most practical way to assure true-breeding for a few plants is hand pollination. Corn is wind pollinated. If you raise only one type (or have only one type tasseling) and no one in your neighborhood has any tasseling at that time, there is no problem. Wind pollination will do fine, for few pollen grains from other strains will reach the silks of your corn.

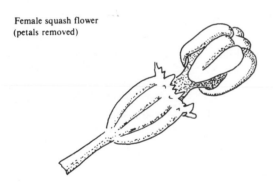

Female squash flower
(petals removed)

If this is not the case, you will need to hand pollinate. Select several of the best corn plants of the same variety and mark them. Before the silks appear, cover each developing ear with a paper sack, tying the sack down so it will stay on. As pollen starts being shed from the tassels, break off a tassel, uncover an ear of another plant that has silks developed, brush the shedding tassel over the silks and reattach the sack. Continue until all ears have been pollinated. Allow corn to mature and dry on the plants. Remove, shuck, and allow to dry further, but protected from birds, mice, etc. Remove the thoroughly dry grains from ears for storage. (This method is used for popcorn, too.)

Muskmelon, cucumber, squash, pumpkins and eggplant are also customarily hand pollinated since the plants are rather large for caging. In each case select the plants to be crossed and mark them. In these plants, except for eggplant, there are separate staminate (male) and pistillate (female) flowers. The latter will be recognized by the small fruit-like body at the base of the flower. Observe female buds to find out when they will open and the day before you plan to pollinate, fasten together the petals with a rubber band, string or other device or enclose the bud in a sack.

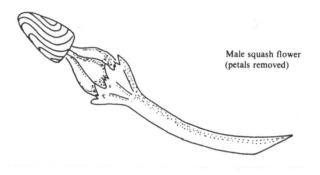

Male squash flower
(petals removed)

The next day, pick a male flower from another plant, remove its petals and brush the anthers (which release the pollen) against the stigma, an enlargement at the tip of the internal parts of the pistillate flower. Cover the female flower again and mark it so you will know which fruit to save seeds from. The eggplant is treated in the same way except that the flowers have both stamen and pistil. As in the other cases, however, it is considered best to cross pollinate even though self pollination is frequent in eggplant. All of these should have the fruit to mature completely and then be handled as indicated elsewhere for tomatoes.

A number of annuals (broccoli, mustard, Chinese cabbage, lettuce, radish and spinach) require either that no plants with which they may cross be flowering at the same time in the neighborhood (isolation or alternate plantings) or that the plants be raised in insect-proof cages. Since broccoli is a quite large plant and will not cross with anything except the other cole plants (common cabbage, kohlrabi, kale, cauliflower, Brussels sprouts and collards) you may treat it separately. That is, if none of the other cole plants are blooming simultaneously with the broccoli or if any that are blooming are caged to keep out insects, just let nature take her course and when the seed pods are almost dry, collect them by cutting off the seed heads. Allow the pods to complete their drying and then collect the seeds by rubbing the dry fruits between your hands and then separate the lighter chaff from the seeds (winnowing) by blowing or wind. (Collards, cabbage, cauliflower, broccoli, Brussels sprouts, radish, kale, kohlrabi, turnips and rutabagas all have fruits that split open when completely dry. The seedstalks therefore must be collected before this occurs.)

The other plants in the group, and your broccoli, if you like, should be caged to avoid cross pollination. A cage large enough to house five to ten plants should be constructed of screen wire. The plants selected should be completely enclosed by the cage and flies introduced into it. (The easiest way to do this is to expose a bit of fresh meat or fish or even dead insects or earthworms so flies lay eggs on them. Then place this in the cage and the flies that develop will not have any pollen except that of the plants in the cage.) Allow the seeds to mature. Cut off the seed stalks and allow them to dry further. Thresh, winnow and store in glass or metal containers. Avoid plastic since occasionally mice will eat through it.

The final group is biennials that are easily cross pollinated, including in some cases crossing with wild relatives. These plants include beets, chard, most cole crops (cabbage, kohlrabi, collards, kale, cauliflower), carrot, parsley, the onion family (onions, chives, leeks), turnips, and rutabagas. The plant, or a part of it, lives over winter and the second summer sends up its flowering stalk. Selection should be made the *first* summer since the characteristics for which we select are obvious then. Enough plants should be saved that any losses during the winter will not deplete the stock and a second selection can be made in the spring. The beets, chard, parsley, carrots, chives, turnips, and rutabagas may be overwintered in the garden protected by mulch, provided mice will not bother them. All may be stored in sand in a cellar, with the roots and bud intact, or in various other ways

people store these vegetables for winter use. In the spring a second selection is made and the plants returned to the garden before the last frost. From this time on the treatment is the same as the other caged plants.

In every case use several plants, the best non-hybrids available. The seeds should be stored in glass or metal containers so insects and rodents can not reach them, each variety in its own well marked container. Be sure to keep duplicate sets of seeds as a precaution since occasionally one batch will be lost. Seed enough for several years should be kept on hand and tested annually for viability. The easiest way to do this is to place ten seeds on a moist paper or absorbent cloth, roll up and keep moist for several days to see if germination occurs. If fewer than five or six germinate, it is time to raise new seed. For this it is best to use the youngest, most viable seeds you have. Plant an excess of seeds so there will be plenty of plants to choose among even after you have discarded all you consider inferior in any way.

Approximate times you may expect to keep seeds are:

> One year -- Corn, onion family
> Two years -- Carrot, okra, parsley
> Three years -- Beans, peas, pepper, tomato
> Four years - Beet, cole family, Chinese cabbage, mustard, radish, rutabaga, spinach, squash, turnip
> Five years -- Cucumber, eggplant, lettuce, muskmelon, salsify

Storing your seed

> The keys to success in storing seeds are:
> 1. Keep them from insects, mice, etc.
> 2. Keep them cool
> 3. Keep the humidity low.

Metal and/or glass containers are best for isolating seeds from pests. Storage in a refrigerator or even the freezor is often recommended. Keeping the humidity low can be achieved by placing a small bag of fresh powdered milk in each airtight container and replacing it about twice a year.

Important Details ...
You'll be glad you have these

No man is born in possession of the art of living any more than of the art of agriculture; the one requires to be studied as well as the other. A man can no more expect satisfaction from random actions than he can expect a good crop from seeds sown without regard to soil and season.

J.C. Loudon

CHAPTER ELEVEN

Many bits of information needed by every gardener are best presented in tabular form. There are three advantages to separating this material into tables in this special chapter. First, it does not break up the continuity of the discussions. Second, tabular presentations are very conserving of space. And finally, certain information is more readily found in tables than in a discussion.

This chapter brings together information from many sources, much of it not usually included in materials for non-professional gardeners. Though you may refer to these pages only occasionally, you will find in them information you will need to become a master gardener.

The most unusual of the tables, "Nutrient Yields in Intensive Gardening", pp. 64-66, provides, possibly for the first time, estimates of the yield per week of calories and five nutrients that a **good** gardener intensively cultivating a unit of land can expect. In this same table is a figure indicating for each vegetable how much more an **excellent** gardener might expect to harvest. This table provided the information on which the concept of the Very Special Survival Vegetables developed.

Also presented here are seed needs and information necessary when planting, suggested emergency seed supplies, typical NPK values of certain organic fertilizers and instructions for using soil analyses, symptoms and treatments of mineral imbalances, and pH tolerances of most common vegetables. The chapter ends with a list of certain sources of seeds.

Nutrient Yields in Intensive Gardening

Vegetable	Weeks from planting thru harvest	Lbs. per 25 sq. ft.	Ratio excellent to good yield	Yield per 25 square feet per week						Comments
				Calories	Protein (gm)	Calcium (mgm)	Iron (mgm)	Vitamin A (IU)	Vitamin C (mgm)	
Artichoke, Jerusalem	30 (52)	52	2.0	38–400	76	44	19	86	21	Caloric value rises during winter storage.
Asparagus	30 (52)	5	2.0	10	1	9	tr.	360	13	
Beans, lima, bush *	10	4	1.3	670	40	140	12	tr. --	--	Based on dry beans.
Beans, lima, pole *	13	4	1.3	520	31	110	12	tr.	--	
Beans, snap, bush*	10	18	1.5	230	14	400	6	4300	140	
Beans, snap pole *	13	23	1.5	220	13	390	6	4200	130	Harvest over a longer period than bush beans.
Beets	13	28	2.5	290	11	110	5	170	68	Cylindra beets provide about double the yield.
Beets plus greens *	13	55	2.5	420	23	750	23	33,000	230	
Broccoli	12	10	1.4	92	10	300	3	7200	330	Transplants. From seeds, reduce yld/wk by a third.
Brussels sprouts	22	27	1.3	230	25	180	8	2800	510	Later part of harvest after frost.
Cabbage, Chinese (compact heading)	10 (8-12)	48	2.0	300	25	900	12	3200	530	Very great varietal variation.
Cabbage, common	16 (13-19)	48	2.0	290	16	600	5	1600	570	Data based on transplants.
Carrots	14	38	7.2	420	11	370	7	110,000	78	
Cauliflower	13 (11-15)	25	2.9	230	23	220	10	520	680	From transplants.

*Very Special Survival Vegetables.

Nutrient Yields in Intensive Gardening

| Vegetable | Weeks from planting thru harvest | Lbs. per 25 sq. ft. | Ratio excellent to good yield | Yield per 25 square feet per week | | | | | | Comments |
				Calories	Protein (gm)	Calcium (mgm)	Iron (mgm)	Vitamin A (IU)	Vitamin C (mgm)	
Chard, Swiss*	30	101	2.0	350	34	1200	45	92,000	450	Length of harvest very variable; up to yr. long.
Collards*	10	48	2.0	860	78	4400	21	140,000	2000	Harvest extends well into winter; growth period used for calculations.
Corn	14	9	2.0	230	9	8	2	970	23	Based on yellow types; white corn has only a trace of vitamin A.
Cucumbers	13	79	1.8	390	24	660	29	6600	290	
Eggplant	22	27	1.5	110	5	54	3	37	23	Transplants.
Garlic*	16	30	2.0	1000	47	220	11	tr.	110	
Kale*	8	29	1.3	460	50	2100	26	110,000	1500	Used as winter vegetable; growth period about 8 wks.
Kohlrabi	10	34	2.0	320	22	460	6	240	470	Leaves may also be eaten.
Leeks	19	120	2.0	780	33	780	16	570	250	Transplants.
Lettuce, head	12	38	2.0	180	12	270	7	4400	88	Transplants may be used to reduce time.
Lettuce, leaf	10 (6-13)	51	2.7	260	19	990	21	28,000	270	Transplants may be used to reduce time.
Muskmelon ("Cantaloupe")	16	18	2.0	75	2	35	1	8500	81	
Mustard*	11	56	1.2	500	49	2000	49	110,000	1600	
Okra	21	15	2.0	100	7	260	2	1400	87	
Onions, bunching	17	50	2.7	460	19	650	13	26,000	410	Most nutrients are in green portions.
Onions, regular	21	50	2.7	370	15	260	5	380	100	Sets or plants. Torpedo onions yield about twice as much. Vit. A for yellow onions.

Nutrient Yields in Intensive Gardening

Vegetable	Weeks from planting thru harvest	Lbs. per 25 sq. ft.	Ratio excellent to good yield	Yield per 25 square feet per week						Comments
				Calories	Protein (gm)	Calcium (mgm)	Iron (mgm)	Vitamin A (IU)	Vitamin C (mgm)	
Parsley	30	13	2.0	87	7	400	12	17,000	340	
Parsnips *	17	60	2.0	1000	23	680	9	420	220	Vit. C drops with storage.
Peas, English *	10 (9-18)	13	2.0	190	14	60	4	1500	62	Much of season is prior to major growing season.
Pepper, Cayenne	27	6	1.6	94	4	29	1	22,000	370	Transplants. Seeds used. Nutrient values without seeds 20-50% lower.
Pepper, green	27	21	1.6	63	3	25	2	1200	370	Transplants. If seeds are eaten or peppers are red, values are higher.
Potato, Irish *	9 (9-14)	50	3.0	1500	43	140	12	tr.	410	Vit. C value is average; value drops in storage.
Radish, common	5	50	2.7	490	29	860	29	300	740	
Rutabaga*	12	100	2.4	1500	35	2100	12	19,000	1400	
Salsify*	17	100	2.7	160-1000	36	590	19	120	140	Calorie values rise during storage.
Soybeans (dry) *	13	4	–	560	48	315	12	110	–	
Spinach*	15 (6)	25	2.3	350	44	1300	42	110,000	700	Growing season includes part of winter.
Squash, yellow bush	12	19	2.0	130	8	190	3	2800	150	
Squash, winter	13	25	1.9	310	9	140	4	23,000	83	Vit. A increases in storage.
Squash Zucchini	11	80	1.5	530	38	880	12	10,000	590	Vit. A is in skin, not flesh.
Sweetpotato *	17	41	3.0	1000	15	280	6	78,000	190	
Tomato	16	49	2.2	300	15	180	7	12,000	360	Eaten unpealed.
Turnip, with tops *	7 (12)	50	1.8	1600	110	7800	64	210,000	4800	Some season assumed before and after normal gardening period.

Note: In the "Weeks Planting to Harvest" column, only the gardening season is considered in calculations of crop occupancy, total occupancy being given in parentheses. In the case of year-long occupancy, as by asparagus and Jerusalem artichokes, the 30 week growing season is assumed for purposes of calculations. Most yields have been calculated from data from "How to Grow More Vegetables..." by John Jeavons. The same source is the basis for the column "Ratio of Excellent to Good Yields" which indicates the multiplier to be used to convert yields expected by a good, experienced gardener to those which might be expected by an exceptional gardener when both use intensive gardening technics. Times of garden occupancy are based on personal experience and on publications concerning gardening in the Southeastern United States. The "Handbook of Nutritional Contents of Foods" (USDA Handbook #8) was used for food analyses.

Hypothetical 1000 sq. ft. Survival Garden Meeting One Person's Nutrient Needs

Vegetable	Area (Sq. Ft.)	Approximate planting date	Harvest Pounds	Harvest Calories (x1000)	Comments
Beans, lima, bush	50	4/15	25	14	For fresh use and preserving
	50	7/1	25	14	
	50	8/1	25	14	
Beans, lima, pole	75	4/15	38	21	May be planted with corn
	75	5/15	38	21	
	75	6/15	38	21	
	75	7/15	38	21	
Beets	5	2/15	11	1	Use roots and greens
	5	3/15	11	1	
	5	4/15	11	1	
	5	5/1	11	1	
	5	8/1	11	1	
	5	8/25	11	1	
	5	9/15	11	1	
Collards	10	2/15	20	4	
	10	3/15	20	4	
	5	4/1	10	2	
	5	8/1	10	2	
	15	9/1	30	6	
	25	9/15	49	9	
Corn	75	4/15	25	9	Not a V.S.S.V.; no extra space requirement when planted with beans or soybeans
	75	5/15	25	9	
	75	6/15	25	9	
	75	7/15	25	9	
Kale	25	2/15	29	4	
	25	9/1	29	4	
Peas, green or snowpeas	100	2/1	53	20	
Potato, Irish	100	2/1	200	56	First planting a rapid grower; last two, good keepers
	150	8/1	300	84	
	150	8/15	300	84	
Radish	40	2/1 to 11/1	40	3	Not a V.S.S.V. but takes no extra space and serves as living mulch
Rutabaga	10	2/15	40	7	
	10	3/15	40	7	
	20	8/15	80	14	Last planting for winter use
	30	9/15	120	21	
Salsify	10	2/1	40	8	
Soybeans	400	5/15	69	127	Plant with corn
Spinach	30	1/15	30	3	
	20	2/15	20	2	
	20	9/1	20	2	
	10	9/15	10	1	
Sweetpotato	25	4/15	41	17	First planting rapid grower; last a good keeper
	50	5/10	82	34	
	125	6/1	205	86	
Turnips	25	1/15	100	9	For roots and greens
	25	2/15	100	9	
	25	3/15	100	9	
	25	4/15	100	9	
	25	8/10	100	9	
	50	9/1	200	18	
	25	9/15	100	9	

This hypothetical garden is for the Carolinas' Piedmont. Planting times will differ from place to place even in this region. It is assumed that food for winter will be preserved by canning or drying and that a number of crops (as beets, collards, kale, rutabaga, spinach and turnips) will be protected in the garden by mulching or in a cold frame during the winter. Estimated yields are generally those for "good gardeners" in the experience of John Jeavons as indicated in his book, *"How to Grow More Vegetables..."*

In practice, more frequent plantings using smaller spaces would use both time and space more efficiently since replanting would be more rapid with less time between successive crops.

Corn, though not a V.S.S.V., is used to provide an additional high calorie food. Grown with soybeans or pole beans, the added calories are produced with no extra space and little less in productivity of the legume.

Suggested Minimum Emergency Supply of Seeds

Vegetable	Amount per person Ounces	Amount per person Grams
*Beans, lima, bush	40-140	1100-4000
*Beans, lima pole	45-160	1300-4500
*Beans, snap, bush	8	225
*Beans, snap, pole	8	225
*Beets	2	55
Broccoli	0.005	0.14
Brussels sprouts	0.005	0.14
Cabbage, Chinese	0.005	0.14
Cabbage, common	0.005	0.14
Carrots	0.05	1.4
Cauliflower	0.005	0.14
*Chard, Swiss	0.005	0.14
*Collards	0.01	0.3
Corn	10.	300.
Cucumbers	0.01	0.3
Eggplant	0.005	0.14
*Kale	0.02	0.6
Kohlrabi	0.01	0.3
Lettuce (mixed)	0.01	0.3
Melons	0.02	0.6
*Mustard	0.02	0.6
Okra	0.06	1.7
Onion	0.01	0.3
Parsley	0.002	0.06
*Peas	10.	280.
Pepper	0.005	0.14
*Potato, Irish	Preserve as potatoes, stored or in ground. Seeds available in 1982.	

Vegetable	Amount per person Ounces	Amount per person Grams
Radish	0.1	3.
*Rutabaga	0.3	9.
*Salsify	1.	28.
*Soybeans	50.	1400.
*Spinach	0.2	6.
Squash, summer	0.3	9.
Squash, winter	0.3	9.
*Sweetpotato	Store as tubers or keep as houseplants.	
Tomato	0.01	0.3
*Turnip	1.	28.

*Very Special Survival Vegetables.

Application. The amounts of viable seeds of the Special Survival Vegetables (marked *) are sufficient for planting for one person for two years with some to spare. Other seeds should be selected as the basis for gardening to supplement or complement these and other foods that are available. The stock should be used but also maintained at this or a higher level as a preparedness measure.

Spacing, Arrangement, Depth of Planting, Emergence Times for Common Vegetables

Vegetable	Spacing (Inches)	Hills	Beds	Double row	Fence or stake	Planting depth (Inches)	Emergence time (Days)
Beans, bush, lima	6		X			1-2	7-10
Beans, pole, lima	10			X	X	1-2	7-10
Beans, bush snap	4		X		X	1-2	7-10
Beans, pole snap	8			X		2-3	7-10
Beets	4		X			1/2	5-10
Broccoli	18		X			1/4	5-10
Brussels sprouts	18		X			1/4	5-10
Cabbage, common	18		X			3/8	5-10
Cabbage, Chinese	5-15*		X			3/8	5-10
Carrot	3		X			1/2	6-10
Cauliflower	15		X			3/8	5-10
Chard	3-10*		X			1	5-10
Corn	12			X		2	3-8
Cucumber	15	X			X	1	3-8
Eggplant	18		X			1/2	5-12
Kale	5-15*		X			1/2	5-10
Kohlrabi	4		X			1/2	4-10
Lettuce	3-15*		X			1/2	3-10
Muskmelon	12			X	X	1	5-10
Mustard	3-12*		X			1/4	3-10
Okra	12			X		1	7-5
Onion, spring	1		X			1/2	4-12
Onion, for bulbs	4		X			1/2	4-12
Parsnip	5		X			3/4	12-17
Parsley	6		X			1/2	12-20
Peas, bush	4-5			X		1	6-35
Peas, pole	5-6			X	X	1	6-35
Pepper	12-15	X				1/4	7-12
Potato	12-15		X			-	-
Radish	2-3		X			1/2	3-10
Rutabaga	6-8		X			1/2	4-10
Salsify	4		X			1	-
Soybeans	4			X		1	5-10
Spinach	3-6*		X			1	6-30
Squash, bush	15-30	X				1	5-10
Squash, vine	30	X			X	1	5-10
Sweetpotato	15-20		X	X		-	-
Tomato	18			X	X	1/4	6-10
Turnip	3-6*		X			1/2	2-5

*Lettuce, kale, spinach, turnips and other leafy plants may be planted thickly and the thinnings used as the wider spacing is developed for mature plants.

Cold Tolerance and Spring Planting

Group A: Very cold hardy. First planting 4 to 6 weeks before expected last spring frost. Asparagus, broccoli, Brussels sprouts, common cabbage, collards, kale, kohlrabi, mustard, onions, parsley, peas, Irish potatoes, radish, rutabaga, salsify, spinach, turnips.

Group B: Cold hardy. First planting 2 weeks before last expected spring frost. Beet, Chinese cabbage, carrot, cauliflower, chard, lettuce, parsnip.

Group C: Warm-season crop, sensitive to frost. First planting the week of last expected frost. Snapbeans, corn, tomato.

Group D: Very cold sensitive. First planting 2 weeks after last frost. Limabeans, cucumbers, eggplant, muskmelon (cantaloupe), pepper, squash, sweetpotato, Irish potato if from seed.

Late Summer or Fall Planting Dates for Most Rapidly Maturing Varieties of Typical Garden Vegetables

Vegetable	Minimum weeks before first expected frost	Vegetable	Minimum weeks before first expected frost
Bean, lima	11	Spinach	9*
Bean, snap	12	Squash, summer	12
Beet	11*	Squash, winter	15
Broccoli	14*	Rutabaga	13*
Brussels sprouts	17*	Tomato	16
Cauliflower	13*	Turnip	7*
Cabbage, Chinese	12*		
Cabbage, common	14*		
Carrot	12*		
Chard	10*		
Collards	14*		
Corn	14		
Cucumber	12		
Kale	14*		
Lettuce, looseleaf	11*		
Mustard	12*		
Peas	10*		
Potato	12		
Radish	6*		

Note: Data for only the most rapidly maturing varieties have been used for this table. Longer lead times will be required for most varieties. Time includes germination period at summer temperatures, period to maturation with about two weeks for slower fall growth due to shorter day lengths, and harvest time. Vegetables marked with an asterisk may have the harvest period extended into the winter by protective mulch or coldframe. Especially if cold-resistant varieties are chosen, they may even continue slow growth unprotected in areas of the South where temperatures seldom fall more than a few degrees below freezing.

Vegetable Transplants

Vegetable	Easily transplanted even with bare roots	Intermediate	Difficult – use pots or peatpots	Transplant growing time (weeks)
Broccoli	X			6
Brussels sprouts	X			6
Cabbage, common	X			6
Cauliflower	X			6
Chard*	X			5
Collard	X			6
Corn*		X		3
Cucumber*			X	3
Eggplant		X		5
Kohlrabi*	X			3
Lettuce*	X			3
Muskmelon*			X	3
Okra*			X	4
Onion		X		10
Pepper			X	5
Squash*			X	3
Sweetpotato	X			5
Tomato	X			6

*Though sometimes transplanted, usually seeded directly in garden.

Maximum Root Depths.

Group A: Shallow rooted: up to 2 feet. Broccoli, Brussels sprouts, cabbage (common), cauliflower, collard, corn, kohlrabi, lettuce, onion, parsley, potato, radish, spinach.

Group B: Intermediate root depths: up to 3 to 4 feet. Beans (snap), beet, carrot, chard, cucumber, eggplant, muskmelon, mustard, peas, pepper, rutabaga, squash (summer), turnip.

Group C: Deep rooted: 4 or more feet. Beans (lima), parsnip, squash (winter), sweetpotato, tomato.

Area and Seed Needs per Planting per Person

Note: It is assumed the gardener is selecting vegetables for a typical home garden to complement foods from other sources. Generous amounts of the smaller seeds are indicated so the most vigorous plants may be selected. (The V.S.S.V. are indicated by asterisks.)

Vegetable	Space (sq. ft.)	Seed per planting			Vegetable	Space (sq. ft.)	Seed per planting		
		Number	Ounces	Grams			Number	Ounces	Grams
*Beans, lima, bush	10	40	1	28	Kohlrabi	1	10	0.002	0.04
*Beans, lima, pole	10	30	0.7	20	Lettuce	5	100	0.004	0.1
*Beans, snap, bush	10	40	0.4	11	*Mustard	5	50	0.003	0.1
*Beans, snap, pole	10	30	0.3	9	Okra	15	30	0.06	2
*Beets	2	40	0.03	0.7	Onion	2	30	0.004	0.1
Broccoli	4	6			Parsley	1	25	0.001	0.04
Brussels sprouts	4	10			*Parsnips	5	200	0.02	0.5
*Butterpeas	15	75	1	28	*Peas, green or snow	20	100	1.3	37
Cabbage, Chinese	2	10			Pepper	2-4	10	0.002	0.06
Cabbage, common	4	10			*Potato, Irish				
Carrots	2	100	0.004	0.1	Spring	20	20eyes		
Cauliflower	2	10			Fall	50	50eyes		
*Chard	2	10	0.06	1.8	Radish		100	0.04	1.1
*Collards	20	50	0.006	0.16	*Rutabaga	3	25	0.02	0.6
Corn	5	10	0.07	2	*Salsify	15	200	0.01	0.3
Cucumber	3	8			*Soybean	30	200	1	28
Eggplant	4	10	0.002	0.04	*Spinach	5	125	0.04	1.3
*Garlic	2	–	4	100	Squash, summer	5	5	0.03	0.7
*Kale	20	100	0.01	0.3	Squash, winter	10-20	10	0.05	1
					*Sweetpotato	10	5 plants		
					Tomato	10	15	0.001	0.04
					*Turnips	5	50	0.003	0.1

Life Cycles and Isolation Requirements for Vegetable Seed Stock Maintenance

Vegetable	Life cycle	Pollination	Isolation requirement
Beet	Biennial	Wind	Varieties only
Bean	Annual	Self	None (Note 1)
Broccoli	Annual	Insect	Isolate from all blooming cole plants (Notes 2 & 3)
Brussels sprouts	Biennial	Insect	Isolate from all blooming cole plants (Notes 2 & 3)
Cabbage, common	Biennial	Insect	Isolate from all blooming cole plants (Notes 2 & 3)
Cabbage, Chinese	Annual	Insect	Isolate from blooming turnips, rutabagas, radish, and horseradish (Note 2)
Cauliflower	Biennial	Insect	Isolate from all blooming cole plants (Notes 2 & 3)
Carrot	Biennial	Insect	Isolate varieties and also from blooming Queen Anne's lace (Note 2)
Collard	Biennial	Insect	Isolate from all blooming cole plants (Notes 2 & 3)
Corn	Annual	Wind	Pollinate by hand or isolate a mile or more
Cucumber	Annual	Insect	Varieties only
Eggplant	Annual	Self or insect	Varieties only (Note 2)
Kale	Biennial	Insect	Isolate from all blooming cole plants (Notes 2 & 3)
Kohlrabi	Biennial	Insect	Isolate from all blooming cole plants (Notes 2 & 3)
Lettuce	Annual	Self & insect	Varieties only (Note 2)
Okra	Annual	Self	None
Onion	Biennial	Insect	Varieties only (Note 2)
Pepper	Annual	Self & insect	Varieties only; hand pollinate
Potato	Annual	——	Tubers are stored over winter; seed-reproduced varieties are being introduced in 1982 (Note 4)
Radish	Annual	Insect	Isolate from mustard, turnip, rutabaga and horseradish (Note 2)
Rutabaga	Biennial	Insect	Isolate from mustard, turnip, radish and horseradish (Note 2)
Spinach	Annual	Wind	Varieties only (Note 2)
Squash	Annual	Insect	Hand pollinate; some varieties will cross
Tomato	Annual	Self	None (Note 1)
Turnip	Biennial	Insect	Isolate from radish, mustard, rutabaga and horseradish (Note 2)

Notes:

1. There may be some crossing even among self-pollinating varieties so an 18-20 foot separation of different varieties is recommended.

2. If two or more of these plants or their varieties are blooming simultaneously, they may be isolated best by caging. Since caging is necessary only during the few days required for pollination, a single cage may be used several times during a season.

3. The cole plants are common cabbage (but not Chinese cabbage), Brussels sprouts, broccoli, cauliflower, kohlrabi, and kale.

4. Until information is available on isolation needs of the new seed-reproduced potatoes, it is advisable to regularly remove any buds developing on nearby potatoes.

Soil Analyses

As soon as possible, even in the fall for a spring garden, take your soil sample and get it evaluated.* To do this you need a representative sample of the topsoil down to one shovel depth. To take this soil sample, dig out six to eight single-scoop holes randomly distributed over the garden area. Clear away top debris (sticks, leaves, etc.) from one side of each hole. Then with the shovel take a slice of soil about a shovel-length deep or down to the subsoil (whichever is less) and an inch thick from beside each hole and mix these samples together thoroughly in a clean container such as a bucket or dishpan. Remove any remaining debris or stones and allow the sample to dry. Consult your local County Agricultural Agent or a farmer's supply store about how to send your sample to have it analyzed. They may have small cardboard containers for this purpose. On page 75, you find how to interconvert conventional and organic fertilizer recommendations.

A quicker alternative is to purchase a small soil analysis kit and use it yourself. The results are comparable with those provided by the laboratory analysis, though not as detailed.

The remainder of the sample should be examined to provide ideas about physical characteristics of your soil. If the soil is dry, moisten a handful very slightly. Mash it into a ball and then mash the ball with a thumb. With the right amount of moisture, the ball should crumble if it is a loamy soil — a mixture of sand, silt and clay. If a ball can not be formed, it is sand or largely sand. If sand is present, when rubbed between thumb and forefinger the grit will be felt. If the soil is primarily silt, it will feel like moist powder. If the sample is largely clay, when wet it will feel slippery, almost like an oiled surface. When a little less moisture is present, it can be worked into shapes as in making brick or pottery. The ideal soil is a loam. (For more details, see p. 26)

*Note: If your soil has different appearances in various parts of your garden you should take a sample for each different area and possibly treat the areas separately. If an unusual area is quite small, you may mix the soils together during soil preparation and so avoid this.

Typical NPK Equivalents of Selected Organic Fertilizers*

Blood, dried	13:2:1
Bone meal, raw	3:22:0
Bone meal, steamed	1:15:0
Cotton seed meal	6:3:1.5
Fish meal	10:6:0
Tankage, animal	8:20:0
Tankage, garbage	2.5:2:1
Peanut meal	7:1.5:1.2
Sludge, sewage	1.5:1.3:0.4
Sludge, activated	6:3:0.2
Soybean meal	7:1.2:1.5
Fish scrap	8:13:4
Manures, fresh	
Cow/steer	0.5:0.3:0.5
Hen	1.1:1.1:0.5
Horse	0.7:0.3:0.7
Sheep	1:0.8:1
Manures, dried	
Cow, east	2:3:3
Cow, west	1:1:2
Chicken	1.5:1.7:2
Sheep	1.5:1.2:2
Hoofmeal; horndust	12.5:1.5:0
Seaweed	1.5:1:5
Wood ashes	0:1.5:8

*Purchased fertilizers may have analyses on the bag. If so, these figures should be used rather than those in the table.

Numbers indicate pounds nitrogen, phosphorus (as P_2O_5) and potassium (as K_2O) per hundred pounds total weight.

When soil is rich it bids defiance to droughts, yields in abundance and of the best quality.

Thomas Jefferson

Application of Soil Analyses to pH Adjustment

pH. Acidity or alkalinity is reported as pH. Very slightly acid (pH about 6.5) is near ideal for most garden plants. Major exceptions are strawberries, blackberries, raspberries and blueberries, all of which require or grow best at a lower pH.

To raise pH 0.5 add agricultural lime, dolomite, or wood ashes as follows:

Light, sandy soil	0.6 lb. per 25 square feet
Sandy loam	0.8 lb. per 25 square feet
Loam	1.2 lb. per 25 square feet
Silt or clay loam	1.4 lb. per 25 square feet

To lower pH by 0.5 add indicated amount of one of the following; or a mixture in these proportions.

Peat	4-5 lbs. per 25 square feet
Compost	25-30 lbs. per 25 square feet
Manure or sludge*	5-8 lbs. per 25 square feet

Double above amounts if the soil has a high organic matter content.

*Note: Any sludge used should be from domestic, not industrial, sewage.

Calculations of Fertilizer Applications from Recommendations Based on Soil Analyses

Recommendation received: Apply 1000 pounds 10:10:10 per acre.

Interpretation: apply 100 pounds of N (Nitrogen), 100 of P (phosphorus as P_2O_5), and 100 pounds of K (potassium as K_2O) per acre or about 0.2 pound of each per 100 square feet, since an acre is about 44,000 square feet. How much of the materials listed would contain 0.2 pound of each of these nutrients?

Example of calculation.

100 pounds of cotton seed meal contains 6 lbs. N, 3 lbs. P and 1.5 lbs. K. (See table, p. 74.)

$$\frac{0.2}{6} \times 100 \text{ or } 3.3 \text{ pounds of cottonseed meal}$$

contains 0.2 pound of N.

It also contains 0.1 lb. P and 0.05 lb. K. Wood ashes (NPK: 0:1.5:8) could be used as a source of K and since we still need 0.15 lb., we calculate:

$$\frac{0.15}{8} \times 100 \text{ or about } 1.9 \text{ lbs. wood ashes}$$

would meet this need and provide about 0.03 lb. P.

Steamed bone meal has little except P (NPK: 1:15:0) so we calculate how much to use to add the extra 0.07 pound (since 0.13 is in the cottonseed meal and ashes combined).

$$\frac{0.07}{15} \times 100 \text{ or about } 0.5 \text{ lb. bonemeal}$$

will fill this requirement and also add a little bit of nitrogen. So you could achieve approximately the recommended fertilization (1000 pounds 10:10:10 per acre) by applying 3.3 lbs. cottonseed meal, 1.9 pounds of wood ashes and 0.5 lb. steamed bone meal per 100 square feet. Especially with the slower acting organic fertilizers the amounts to be applied are not critical. Even though there is considerable variation from sample to sample, estimates such as this are adequate. (It is most convenient to use volumetric measurements in fertilizing. Fortunately, a close enough approximation is to consider a pint (two cups) as equivalent to a pound. These measurements would be simply read off as pints rather than as pounds.)

Corresponding calculations can be made starting with recommended amounts of organic fertilizers. It is generally simpler to begin with inorganic or commercial fertilizer recommendations which provide more directly the weights of elements to be applied. It is because of the ease of calculation that I recommend getting analyses in commercial fertilizer terms.

Mineral Imbalances: Symptoms and Countermeasures

Mineral	Symptoms	Comments
Boron	Deficiency: Buds fail to develop; leaves small, misshapen; stems short, hard. Cauliflower browns; beet blackheart; turnip internal browning.	Most often seen in high pH (above 6.8) soils. Lower pH. (Warning: only very low amounts of boron are needed. Consult Agriculture Agent for recommendations before adding any.)
Calcium	Deficiency: Stunted growth; leaves small, young ones turning yellowish-green. Root and stem tips die. Blossom-end rot in tomatoes; cavity spot of carrots.	Apply lime, dolomite, oyster shells, or basic slag.
Copper	Deficiency: Leaves yellowing but veins remain green. Leaves may be elongated. Onions soft with scales thin and pale yellow.	Usually associated with very high soil organic content, as peat and muck soils, or with alkaline soils.
Iron	Deficiency: Young leaves become distinctly yellow or white between veins. Brown patches develop all over leaves.	Especially seen in soils of pH above 6.8. Lower pH, especially with humus. Use chelated iron.
Magnesium	Deficiency: Yellowing between veins first in older, then in younger, leaves. Older leaves may fall off.	Especially seen in acid soil or in soils having high potassium content. Use dolomite.
Manganese	Deficiency: Young leaves yellowish between veins. Similar to iron deficiency with overall pale appearance. Beets: leaves intensely red. Onions and corn: narrow yellow stripes in leaves.	Most common if pH is above 6.7. Lower pH with humus.
Molybdenum	Deficiency: Leaves very narrow. Plants stunted. Older leaves have yellowing between veins. Edges of leaves turn up and become yellow or brown in tomatoes, bean and cucumbers.	Associated with very acid soils. Add lime, ashes, dolomite, etc.
Nitrogen	Deficiency: Leaves (first older but finally all) pale yellow-green but may be reddish, purple or orange. Leaves small and growth of plant very stunted.	Most common in wet, poorly aerated soils or ones subjected to leaching. Poultry manures, dried blood and fish emulsions provide fast relief. For longer lasting treatment, increase soil humus content especially by raising legumes as green manure crops or use legume hay as a mulch.
	Excess: Plants excessively large, dark green, and slow to flower.	Dig in low-nitrogen materials as fresh leaves and sawdust.

continued

Phosphorus	Deficiency: Older leaves, especially the veins, reddish or purple, starting on lower surfaces. Plants are slow growing with thin, short stems and are slow to mature.	Add bone meal and rock phosphate. In acid soil, also add lime; in alkaline, humus.
Potassium	Deficiency: Older leaves turn yellow then brown ("scorched") at the margins. Chlorotic areas may appear. Symptoms early in lettuce. Leaf tip dieback in onions.	May be due to leaching. Add humus in any form. Wood ashes are a ready source of potassium. Use granite dust, greensand or seaweed mulch.
Sulfur	Deficiency: Younger leaves have lighter than normal veins.	Increase soil humus content.
Zinc	Deficiency: Leaves long, narrow, yellowish, possibly with dead areas.	Zinc deficiencies are most often seen in soils of very high or very low pH. Manures are a good source for treatment.

Acidity Tolerances of Common Vegetables

Most vegetables grow best within a pH range of about 6.0 to 6.8 but some will tolerate higher pHs (up to about 7.5) and others lower ones. As a rule of thumb, you may expect a tolerance of about 1.5 pH units. pH extremes tend to limit mineral availability so the range will vary with soil mineral content. In addition, the range is generally extended in soils of high humus content (as 5 per cent).

Approximate tolerance range (pH)	Vegetables
6.0-7.5	Beet, broccoli, cabbage (common and Chinese), cauliflower, chard, lettuce, muskmelon, okra, onion, parsnip, salsify, soybean, spinach
5.5-6.8	Beans (various), Brussels sprouts, carrot, collard, corn, cucumber, eggplant, kale, kohlrabi, mustard, peas (various) pepper, radish, rutabaga, squash, tomato, turnip
5.0-6.8	Potato, sweetpotato

Salt Tolerance of Selected Crops In Periods of Rapid Plant Growth*

Least sensitive to most sensitive: Barley, sugarbeets, wheat, sorghum, beets, soybeans, broccoli, spinach, tomato, cabbage, potato, corn, sweetpotato, broadbean, lettuce, bell pepper, onion, carrott, bean, muskmellon

Notes:

(1) Some varieties are more sensitive at one period in development than at others. Germinating seeds may appear especially sensitive because of the higher concentration of salts near the soil surface due to evaporation there.

(2) In addition to the first four or five plants in the list, the following are useful in improving saline soils: Bermuda grass, tall and crested wheat grasses, tall fescue, perennial rye and Hardinggrass.

*Adapted from Leon Berstein, Salt Tolerance of Plants, USDA Agricultural Information Bulletin 283 (1970).

Alkali Tolerant Plants

The following plants are unusually resistant to high pH levels and so may be helpful in improvement of very alkaline soils, including sodic soils:

Oats, barley, alfalfa, sweet and red clovers, beets soybeans.

Relative Shade Tolerances of Certain Vegetables

Shade tolerant: Broccoli, Brussels sprouts, bush beans, edible pod peas, green onions, leaf lettuce, potato, radish, spinach.

Intermediate: Beets, chard, kohlrabi, head lettuce, parsnip, turnip.

Not shade tolerant: Corn, cauliflower, carrot, cucumber, onion for bulbs, peas, peppers, squash, tomato.

As long as key agricultural decisions are primarily economic rather than nutritional and ecological, we will have malnutrition and even starvation.

The Author

Problem Climates and Soils ...

*Current climate
projections indicate
the prospect is one
that should be in the minds
of everyone concerned
about the human race . . .*

John Gribben

CHAPTER TWELVE

Gardening in Subtropical Areas

Many subtropical areas, such as southern Florida, as well as tropical regions are characterized by a two-season year — a wet season and a dry season. In addition to this, such areas often suffer from poor and/or shallow soils with low nutrient levels, sandy soils with little water retention, or limestone or shell-based soils with poor mineral balances. Available iron is almost always low.

With such a multiplicity of challenges, those gardening in subtropical areas will need to apply several sections of this chapter as well as the more general gardening practices in earlier chapters. This particular section will focus on problems relating specifically to season, including high light intensities, very high summer temperatures and the seemingly year-long problems you will have with pests since there is no dramatic winter kill.

Perhaps the easiest response to the problems of subtropical gardening — and probably the one the novice should adopt — is to obtain information on local and regional gardening from the County Extension Agent and also from successful local gardeners. Find from them what varieties of the vegetables you want to grow do well in your particular area and when they plant.

Try these varieties and planting times while adopting the best soil development and plant nurturing methods you can, some of which are discussed elsewhere in this section as well as in chapter 5 (pp. 25-28) and chapter 7 (pp. 39-46).

The general principle you will discover is that much of gardening is backwards in wet-dry season subtropical areas. And this is true in two respects: winter is the major gardening season and warm weather crops such as tomatoes and squash are planted before cold weather crops such as lettuce or spinach.

Next, attempt to extend your garden's growing season a bit. Temperatures may be lowered some degrees by shading during afternoons by planting to the east side of trees or some trellised vines or a fence or house.

High temperatures increase the amount of water required for maintaining plants in good condition. Provide water directly on the ground and take precautions to minimize water loss through evaporation.

During the dry season, you can use drip or seepage irrigation. For this latter, stopper the hole of a large, unglazed crockery flower pot and bury it almost to the rim in the soil of your garden. Keep the pot more or less filled with water and plant close around it. Through seepage, a twelve inch pot may meet the needs of two or possibly more tomato, cucumbers or squash plants. It will care for several times as many lettuce, carrot or beet plants.

As for insects and other pests and diseases, apply the methods discussed in chapter 8 (pp. 47-54) even more intensely than needed in gardens in more temperate zones. Especially emphasize attracting and maintaining the predators you need to keep insects under control. Select the varieties most resistant to the particular problems in your area and rogue out quickly and often any plants that are diseased.

Subtropical and tropical areas are notable for poor soils and diseases and insects often affect more severely those plants already suffering other stresses. Therefore it is very important for you to have tests of your soil, not only for the major nutrients but for minor ones as well and then to correct any deficiencies.

This step in soil improvement will not eliminate diseases and pests but in some cases it will make plants in your garden less likely to be attacked and, what may be more important, it may make attacks less significant. That is, this may serve for damage control when some damage may not be completely eliminated.

Whenever and wherever soil is used at rates greater than its generation that soil is reduced in its potential for supporting life and all future generations are consequently impoverished.

Author Unknown

Too Much Rain

Almost everywhere there are times of too much rain. Even in deserts there are occasional violent rainstorms, usually lasting only minutes. In other areas there may be long wet spells. This section, however, deals with the problem of those living in areas subject to "excessive" rainfall for long periods, as in parts of the tropics and the Pacific Northwest.

The most serious problem is that the high precipitation constantly leaches nutrients, especially nitrogren and potassium, from the soil.

Nature's response to this situation is instructive and hints of counter measures for the gardener.

In areas having moderate rainfall the available nutrient content of the soil is typically several times more than the nutrients in the plants and animals inhabiting the area. In rain forests, the reverse is true. Further, in the latter, as nutrients are released either by washing from the plant surfaces, excretion or decay they are very rapidly recycled into the plants in the area. This is "tight" nutrient cycling.

The question is: How can we apply this information to practical gardening?

In some areas the solution is to imitate the rain forest by developing a mixed garden flora having the following characteristics.

1. There will be a complete plant canopy and a heavy, decayable mulch over the soil year around.

2. Plants will when practical be in two or three "stories", an overstory of tall plants, an intermediate layer and a low-growing group that practically covers the ground.

3. Plants will have a thick mat of roots in the upper portion of the soil and will include some deep rooted plants that will "pump" minerals from the subsoil to the surface.

4. Dead plant parts will be recycled either in place or in a compost heap. (If a compost heap is used it should be partially sheltered from the frequent rains to minimize leaching losses.)

In either case, a constant supply of decayable and decaying organic matter should be maintained throughout your garden so the vigorously growing bacteria, fungi and other organisms can take up minerals before they move too deep for the roots to use them.

5. When any part of the garden is not in use cover crops should be grown with emphasis on legumes.

The idea is illustrated by a garden planted as shown below:

Plant Height	Rooting Depth		
	Deep	Intermediate	Shallow
Tall*	Tomato** Pole Limas**	Cucumbers**	Corn
Intermediate		Bush snapbeans Peppers	
Low		Chard	Lettuce Spinach Radish

*All plants are scattered relatively uniformly throughout the garden, especially the tall or staked ones so light reaches the low-growing plants.

**Staked

NOTE: A cover crop should be planted any time the garden is not in use.

Gardening in Shade, Fog and Overcast Areas

Although many plants do grow in the shade and even will not tolerate full summer sun, almost all agricultural and garden plants do best with full sunlight for at least six or eight hours per day. However, vegetables show a great range of tolerance of shade. (See table on p. 78) Lettuce is one that even does better in the early summer if shaded somewhat for most of the day. In addition to the shade tolerant vegetables mentioned in the table, mints, chives, garlic chives, parsley, thyme and some other herbs thrive in partial shade.

Shade tolerance is relative, however. A factor which diminishes shade tolerance sharply is continual overcast, cloudy or foggy weather. Therefore the range of plants that can be successfully grown in shady areas should be expected to be lower along the New England and Western coasts and also in mountains where cloudy days are common.

In such areas the effect is that growth of many plants is delayed so that times to maturity are increased, often being doubled.

This condition limits the range of vegetables that can be grown in these areas. To some extent, though, gardeners may compensate by choice of more rapidly maturing varieties. County Agricultural Extension Agents and local garden supply centers as well as local, experienced gardeners can be helpful in suggesting choices.

In addition, in small gardens, reflectors have been used successfully to increase the light reaching garden plants, making it possible to grow shade - intolerant plants in an otherwise unsuitable space. In fact, in one experiment both morning and afternoon shading were successfully compensated for by two reflective aluminum surfaces placed appropriately to direct light to the plants. Though probably less practical since the available light is more diffused, a similar arrangement could increase light reaching plants during periods of cloud, fog or overcast skies.

*The times call for a new
land ethic,
a new reverence for the land,
and a better understanding
of our dependence on a
resource
that is too often taken for
granted.*

Lester Brown

Gardening in Mountainous Regions

There are a number of variables associated with mountains of importance to gardeners. The most obvious is that temperatures are inversely related to elevation — the higher you climb the colder it is, on the average, about 1°F for each 300-400 foot rise. In the Rockies, for example, at the highest elevations snow and frost occur year around. In the yet more varied Himalayas, elevation differences are so extreme that subtropical plants may be grown in some lower valleys and perpetual snow — and no gardens — occurs only a few miles away. In a short distance the flora changes from that found in Jacksonville, FL, to that of northern Canada.

There are also great differences in precipitation and water availability associated with different parts of a mountain. Precipitation is greatest near the top, the maximum occurring near the peak on the side of prevailing winds. A rain "shadow" (an area of reduced rainfall) may be found on the downwind side of the mountain and extending many miles from a high range.

One result of the high rainfall of the mountain summit is a lower zone of adequate moisture but also lower rainfall below the summit. In the tropics this is an excellent area for gardens which will be either watered by natural downward seepage or by irrigation from perpetual springs and streams.

Light intensity varies a great deal from place to place in mountains. Toward the equator slopes receive much more sunlight than their polar-facing counterparts. As a result, plant zones on one side of a mountain (in the U.S. the north slope) will often be hundreds of feet lower than on the opposite slope. From a perspective of microclimates, the north slope will be hundreds of miles "farther north" than the south slope.

The above is a long way of saying that the gardener in mountainous areas will find no pat answers to climate-related questions of gardening. Experience and experimenting will be required until an adequate "database" has been developed for the local condition, even for a particular garden. The following suggestions are intended to help you as a gardener to develop such a database for use in a chosen garden spot. Subsequently the information may be used not only for that individual garden but may serve as a reasonable starting point for other gardens nearby.

First, obtain local information from your Agricultural Extension Service and others who are already gardening in your area. This information should include ideas on climatic variations (e.g., first and last frost-free dates) associated with variations in elevation. Find out the expected length of the growing period as estimated between frost periods.

The personal database you develop for your garden should include times of latest spring and earliest fall frosts and comments on each variety of vegetables tried, including its location in the garden.

In higher elevations particularly, fast maturing varieties and those considered adapted for Northern conditions should be tried.

Every effort should be made to keep plants growing vigorously. In the spring this will mean pulling back the mulch a bit and exposing the soil directly to sunlight to raise the temperature rapidly. Cloches or other transparent covers can be used effectively to raise the temperature a bit and to protect plants from late frosts.

Making sure plants have adequate soil moisture is also a part of the program to maintain vigorous growth. Drip and seepage irrigation (p. 80) are especially suited to this situation since runoff should be avoided to help control erosion.

The need for constant vigorous growth so plants can mature on time under frequently adverse conditions also calls for frequent fertilizing. For the true Survival Garden to be maintained with no or at least a minimum of outside input calls for a vigorous composting program, so that fertilizer will be available for frequent applications. The compost in this circumstance has the usual functions of compost but also serves as an absorbent of light so that soil temperatures will rise slightly above those of less dark soils.

If mineral deficiencies are found from soil analyses, the needed nutrients may be supplied via the compost pile or as slow-release fertilizers, or both.

The mountain gardener has a special incentive to use season-extending methods especially those which get the garden off to an early start such as use of a hotbed or coldframe, cloches, and transplants grown indoors.

For the mountain gardener who wants to be most self-sufficient it is even more important than for most gardeners that you be aware of the subtle differences in microclimates from one part of your property to others. A spot shielded from cold spring winds by a south-facing cliff and free from frost for days or even weeks earlier than a nearby area may be ideal as the starting spot for your garden each year.

Gardening in Peaty Soils

Peat is formed from partially decomposed plant remains collected under water. Peaty soils show some evidence of the plants from which they are derived, being fiberous and sometimes having easily recognizable plant parts, such as bits of stem or root.

All sorts of plants can develop into peat if they partially decay under water. In northern areas, sphagnum moss (also called peatmoss) is a major peat former. There and farther south, plants which grow in marshes and swamps serve this function.

Although peaty soils with their dark color appear to be very rich, peats vary considerably in pH and in nutrient content. Peats from sphagnum are quite acid and have very low nutrient contents, as did the peatmoss from which it developed. Peats

formed from other plants are much less acid or about neutral in pH and have higher nutrient levels.

All peaty soils have very high capacities for holding water, typically five to eight times that of loams. In spite of the large amounts of water stored by peats, the amount available to the plants in your garden is only slightly higher than that in loams and up to 25% higher than that in silty loams. This is due to the water binding properties of the plant fibers of the peat.

A disadvantage peat has is that, as long as the water level is high, the soil will remain too wet for most garden plants. For this reason, the first step for you to take in developing a garden in peat areas is to establish drainage.

Once drainage is developed, better access to oxygen will allow more rapid nutrient release and formation of muck from the organic component of the soil. Addition of lime will cause the pH to drift upward for several months if the soil is acid. Neutralization of the acid will improve the balance of nutrients available to your vegetables and will accelerate the conversion of peat to muck.

The developing muck has a high water content so nutrients will readily leach from your soil at this stage. Therefore, applications of slow-release fertilizers are called for. Whether you choose organic or the commercially available pellets, the selection should be made on the basis of your garden soil's specific nutrient deficiencies as revealed in your soil analysis. Slow release fertilizers will provide the missing or deficient nutrients at rates appropriate for plant use without excessive losses.

Another possibility you might try with acid peat soils is to grow "acid-loving" plants such as blueberries.

In areas where peat is close to humus-deficient soils, yet another possibility is to use the peat as an amendment for the mineral soil.

Peats derived from plants other than sphagnum have a fair amount of plant nutrients and so will add both nutrients and humus to soils to which they are applied. Soil amendment using these peats is especially valuable in those areas dominated by soils of glacial origin in the northern states and Canada or in sandy stretches of the coastal plains and in Florida.

Muck Soil

Muck soils, as previously mentioned, are formed from peat when it is drained and thereby subjected to oxidation of its organic matter. While muck is widespread, it is restricted to areas which at one time were swamps or marshes or bogs. Large areas of muck were once found in Florida, in the lower coastal plains of the East Coast, and in formerly glaciated areas. Unfortunately, much of this valuable soil has been depleted by inappropriate farming methods which do not foster humus conservation or replenishment consistent with the loss.

Muck should be clearly distinguished from peat and from moist clay. As long as the soil has a fibrous texture due to the presence of remnants of its plant origin, the soil is a peat. Once these have broken down it is muck. Just as the terms peat and muck are often confused, clay soils are sometimes incorrectly spoken of as muck. Their inorganic origin is quite different from that of true muck.

The oxidation which converts peat to muck both releases plant nutrients and increases the capacity of the soil to store these in readily available forms. In addition, muck usually has a number of physical characteristics which are favorable to plant growth, such as pore spaces, aeration and water holding capacity.

In mucky as in peaty soils, drainage is essential for successful gardening or farming, but drained muck also has two unfortunate features. It is subject to much more rapid oxidation than humus replacement. Unless care is taken, ultimately so much organic matter may be lost that the soil is no longer productive without heavy fertilization. Its only function is to hold the plants in place.

Since dry muck is unusually light, it is very subject to wind erosion. Losses of an inch in depth per year are common, so some muck soils are depleted in only a generation or so.

If you are a gardener working for a sustainable system you certainly do not want to see your garden reduced to unproductive plots. Fortunately, there are measures which can slow the process of degradation and lead to a sustainable, though lower level of soil humus.

... everything has a source in the land or sea, and we must respect these sources.

Thor Heyerdahl

The first step to this end is to maintain an actively decaying mulch at all possible times over exposed areas of your garden. The resulting continuous replacement of the decomposing humus will finally result in a soil with an organic content which can be maintained in your climate. Mulching also helps prevent wind erosion.

Suppose in your area the major readily available source of mulch is lawn clippings. These are useful if applied in thin layers and "fluffed up" at intervals of several weeks. They are also an especially good component of a mulch that includes leaves or straw.

After drainage has been established, clay may be added to muck as a soil amendment and mineral source, although the cost and effort may be high.

The water level may be allowed to rise when the garden is not in use and later maintained as high as possible without interfering with your gardening. These steps will minimize oxidation of the soil and wind erosion.

Mucky soils should be carefully monitored for available plant nutrients. Especially if the muck was formed from sphagnum moss, as in northern bogs, the initial nutrient content is quite low. This situation may be changed as mineral soil is incorporated into the muck but there is always the chance — even a probability — that some essential elements will be low or missing from the combination and have to be added. The advice of a soil analyst should be sought and this is another occasion when the slow-release fertilizers are appropriate.

Hardpan or Pan

Pan is a layer of hard, compact and less permeable soil with layers below it and above it that are more easily penetrated. It it usually only a few inches thick and often results when soil is cultivated at times when a clay subsoil is too moist.

Pan may also be produced in arid regions by natural processes or by poor irrigation practices. It may form when finer soil particles move from higher soil layers and fill in soil spaces. Pan also forms when slightly soluble salts are deposited on soil particles and cement them together.

In any case, pan limits root development to the shallower soil layer, thereby leading to poor growth of plants.

Temporary relief from hardpan is often a mechanical problem, since the hard layer is usually only a few inches thick and often only eight to twelve inches below the surface. A subsoil plow that breaks (but does not "turn") the soil to a depth of perhaps 18 to 24 inches will break up the hardpan and allow roots to penetrate to the underlying, more favorable soil. With doubledigging (p. 27) the hardpan will be broken through and should present no further problem.

Whether the temporary treatment will be enough depends on the reason the hardpan developed in the first place. If it was due to poor agricultural practices, changes of these methods will be effective in prevention of further problems.

Since the Survival Garden covers only small land areas, the temporary treatment may be repeated every few years if hardpan formation should continue in spite of the gardening methods used. It is more likely, however, that there will be no more problem. Except for poor agricultural methods, hardpan is associated with an insufficiency of water to move the leached materials to the groundwater or to soil below root level.

In the Survival Garden in humid areas, once the hardpan is broken up the remaining clods will gradually break down through root action and weathering. In more arid regions, sufficient irrigation above that required to replace evaporative losses of water should be sufficient to prevent a recurrence of the problem and finally lead to breakdown of the hard clumps.

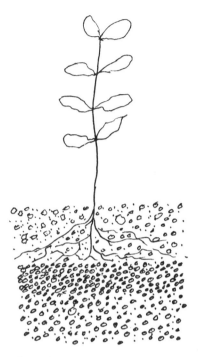

Root development with hardpan

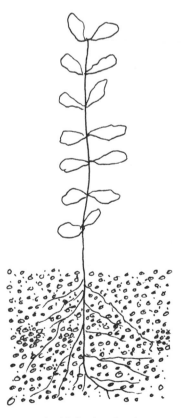

... and with broken hardpan

Alkaline and Saline Soils

Several conditions lead to alkaline and saline soils and treatments appropriate for one may be completely inappropriate for another. Some major types of such soils are considered here.

High-lime soils. High lime soils having a pH of about 8.0 to 8.4 are found in humid areas such as parts of Florida where much of the underlying material is limestone or sea shell-based. They contain up to about 10 percent calcium carbonate but only low concentrations of soluble salts. Gardening problems are primarily the results of excessive moisture and deficiencies of plant nutrients associated with these soils.

Drainage is needed to improve the productivity of high-lime soils. Drainage alone, however, is not the answer. With few exceptions, these soils are deficient in one or more plant nutrients, another reason for soil testing. Also, at high pH levels of 8.0 to 8.4 plant responses to nutrient availability are not the same as those at the more desirable pH range of 6.5 to 7.0. At the higher levels, an application of

Perhaps the best kept secret of the 20th Century, in working with the land people are more productive than machinery.

Harold Gilliam

nutrients which might have resulted in a spurt of growth in one variety of vegetables may invoke unfavorable reactions in another. This being the case, at these high levels of alkalinity the growing of several plants close together or in quick succession, as suggested elsewhere, is often not feasible.

But what gardener wants to be restricted to growing just corn or beans or lettuce or tomatoes? He wants all from the same soil and in the same season.

The most obvious solution to the high pH problem with high-lime soils (the addition of gypsum or sulfur or both to lower the pH) unfortunately does not work in this situation. A slower, but in the long run more effective treatment is the use of manures which will have four desirable effects: Manures will tend to neutralize the alkali and so lower the pH; they will provide a wide variety of trace minerals which are often deficient in these soils; they are a good source of potassium in available form, a major nutrient usually in short supply in high-lime soils; and they improve the nutrient holding capacities and texture of these soils.

With drainage and fertilization based on the deficiencies of the particular plot, high-lime soils can be brought to a high level of productivity.

In a Survival Garden, which requires only small amounts of space, in those areas where various soil types are in close proximity, the high-lime soils may also be amended to advantage by mixing in other soils along with manures.

Sodic soils. Of all naturally occurring soil types, sodic soils, which are found in desert and semi-desert areas, are among the most difficult and expensive to bring into productive use for agriculture. These soils have very little soluble salts but very high levels of sodium ions which results in a pH above 8.5. Fortunately for the home gardener, sodic soils are usually in particular spots and there will be some saline and normal soil areas nearby. Most gardeners will be wise to avoid staking out even a small garden in these spots. If this cannot be arranged, a competent soil scientist or others experienced in gardening in sodic soils (as the County Agricultural Agent) should be consulted for advice before abandoning hope of having a garden.

Some general procedures that can be helpful are the use of gypsum or sulfur to lower the pH, mixing this in with the soil as thoroughly as possible; the adding of organic materials to improve the soil structure; and the growing of any possible plants in order to open up the soil. Such plants may include native plants as well as others indicated as alkali tolerant in the table on page 78.

Saline Soils. Saline soils have a high content of sodium chloride or other soluble salts. The pH is usually in range 7.0 to 8.5, depending on just what salts are present. The white alkali areas of the West which have white crusts in dry weather periods but not after rains are saline soils. True saline soils (in marked contrast with saline-sodic soils) are relatively easy to treat.

The first step in treatment of saline soils is to establish drainage. The white alkali area is one in which salts accumulate through evaporation of ground water or water flowing in from nearby higher ground. Hence almost by definition they will present a drainage problem. Once drainage is provided, the salts can be leached from the soil by either rain or irrigation.

One method of leaching is to mulch the area heavily enough to prevent plant growth and to prevent surface evaporation. Rainfall will then usually be sufficient to leach out the salts since water movement will always be downward in this circumstance.

Once treated, if saline soils are to remain productive, the amount of irrigation plus natural precipitation must be in excess of that required simply to replace evaporative losses of water. As in any garden, this amount can be diminished by measures which lower evaporation, including shielding from prevailing winds and mulching.

Saline-sodic soils. The fact that saline-sodic soils often look like simple saline soils is a special reason for emphasizing soil tests for the areas where they both occur — dry regions of the West. Sometimes they can be told apart by the fact that saline-sodic soils may have black crusts because of organic matter dissolved at the high pH — hence the name black alkali. Saline-sodic soils are like saline soils in having high concentrations of soluble salts (which is not characteristic of sodic soils) as well as the high proportion of sodium ions found in sodic soils. Because of high sodium content, the pH is usually in the range of 8.0 to 8.5.

Saline-sodic soils, however, can be made quite productive if first treated with either gypsum or sulfur so that the sodium ions are removed. Gypsum is usually chosen for this because of its more rapid action. The use of sulfur depends on slower, microbial activity.

Leaching to remove the soluble salts **follows** the gypsum or sulfur or mixed soil treatment.

Important note: Leaching **prior to** (rather than after) removal of the excess sodium ions converts saline-sodic soils to sodic — a counter productive measure. For this reason it is especially important that the soil be evaluated very carefully before treatment starts and also that sufficient time be permitted for the soil amendment to be completed before leaching is undertaken. Once saline-sodic soils are properly treated, if the cause of salinization is avoided, they can be quite productive.

What has gone wrong, probably, is that we have failed to see ourselves as part of a large and indivisible whole ... We have failed to understand that the earth does not belong to us, but we to the the earth.

Rolf Edberg

*Soil is the raw material
of agriculture.
We can pave it,
or we can save it,
knowing that whatever
choice we make
will profoundly influence
the lives of unborn
generations.*

Gus Speth

Gardening in Adobe and Clay Soils

Adobe and clay soils are usually very rich in plant nutrients but have poor physical characteristics. They are often impervious to rain and have too fine spaces for good root development. Such soils, once moistened, hold large amounts of water but much of it is not available to plants.

It is a common belief that adobe soils are hopeless for growing vegetables. If you live in an adobe soil area, you can have a Survival Garden. Properly handled, such soils may quickly provide the basis for an excellent garden.

The most generally applicable treatment is the development of a high humus content of the soil through manuring, addition of compost and heavy mulching.

The function of the humus is to aggregate the clay or clay and silt particles together to provide "crumb" — the large particles formed by "gluing together" small soil particles. The decaying organic materials at the same time continuously make minerals from decaying matter and from clay particles available for solution in the soil moisture. From the soil solution they are readily absorbable by roots and root hairs. As elsewhere, but especially in adobe soil areas that are subject to extremely high summer temperatures, the mulch helps cool the soil and keeps it from "baking."

Gardening in Sandy Soil

Sandy soil has three deficiencies: It has a low content of minerals both in absolute terms and as available nutrients; it has a low capacity for holding water so that it is available to plants; and its buffering capacity is very limited.

Anyone making careful observations of plants growing in extremely sandy soil quickly realizes that the assemblages differ sharply from those found in nearby loam or clay soils. Conditions in sand are simply too extreme for most garden plants to thrive unless special attention is given to their needs.

The current most common practice is to treat the sand, in effect, as a rooting medium and to use basically hydroponic methods, i.e., large amounts of commerical fertilizers are applied along with frequent irrigation.

A suggestion for a less energy-intensive gardening method for sandy soils is provided by the observation that in newly-cleared sandy soils there is often a high concentration of humus.

Addition of humus and decaying organic materials does not provide silt and clay but it does improve the water holding capacity and available mineral supply. Therefore this step — manuring, adding compost or domestic sludge and mulching with readily decaying materials — will greatly improve sand or sand-rich soils.

In small gardens the addition of silt and clay (or simply any sand-poor soil) to sand is feasible if the source of it is nearby. If this is attempted, one or two pounds of clay and twice as much silt applied once or twice a year over each square foot will be slowly incorporated into the soil. At the same time, compost should be applied and the surface should be kept well mulched as much of the time as practical. This provides a continuous supply of food for the soil-building organisms and also keeps the soil temperature low. (Note graph on p. 38)

How to Improve Soil if Manure, Domestic Sludge, Compost and Mulch Are Unavailable

In most areas where anyone would home-garden, some organic materials that are useful as soil additives and mulch are available at low cost and/or with relatively little work. What can you do if this is not the case? Must you give up completely the idea of organic or more natural gardening and stay with or convert to the use of inorganic commercial fertilizers?

If you want to be able to raise your own vegetables in such a situation, expect a period of preparation of several years duration. This is a case in which planning for the future will pay off. Anticipatory action is the name of the game.

Organic soil additives can be purchased, of course, but those brought from great distances are expensive. In most cases a reasonable alternative is to grow a green manure, starting with a crop such as millet or sorghum which has a very low moisture requirement. In many areas, two or three different green manure crops can be grown each year and the whole be incorporated in the soil when maximum growth has occurred but before the plants themselves die.

This is one time when application of commercial "chemical" fertilizers should be fitted into the gardening technic. Applied in small but frequent doses, such fertilizers, especially if mixed with some source of a wide range of minerals, such as manure or seaweed, will greatly speed up the process of soil development.

By such means, even without "chemical" fertilizers, novelist and farmer William Faulkner states he could restore poor ground in only seven years simply by incorporating crop residues in the soil.

Considering commercial inorganic fertilizers, from an economic perspective alone the greatest efficiency in fertilization in most American soils at present is the combining of inorganic chemicals with application of organic materials that raise soil humus content. And the greatest efficiency of plant production per pound of bought fertilizer is usually achieved at the lowest levels of application of such combinations.

Nature can not be ordered about except by obeying her.
Sir Francis Bacon

The danger for modern man is that he will reduce the earth to a desert ... introducing death where God wishes life.
Pope John Paul I

Oregano

Bergamot

Thyme

Garlic chives

Peppermint

Tea mint

Bay

Chives

Purslane

Marjoram

Photo-ink print of fresh-picked herbs from the author's garden.

The Many Faces of Herbs ...

...no man or woman can be very miserable that is master of a garden.

John Evelyn

CHAPTER THIRTEEN

Herbs are experiencing a deserved renewed interest. Through the ages they have served many purposes, some now considered fanciful. They have had — and sometimes deserved — popularity as medicinals. They have also served the interesting but unscientific role of love-potions. In the spring herbs provide some home gardeners the boost needed to recover from winter. Many herbs are used as flavorings or as refreshing teas. Several herbs are reputed to repel certain pests and a few have been shown to be effective in pest control in careful experiments.

Herbs, using the term broadly, come in several categories: annuals, biennials, and perennials. The last group includes not only non-woody herbs but, as used here, some shrubs or even small trees.

Most herbs can be started from seed but the perennials are usually started from divisions or cuttings. Although herb seed are widely available, the rarer types are most easily obtained from nurseries that specialize in herbs.

Growing herbs, however, is not just a matter of scratching the soil and tossing out a package of seed, as one might easily assume from the number of herbs that regularly self-seed. The problem is that most herb seed are so small that special precautions are called for in planting them.

Selection of just what herbs to grow is certainly a personal matter. For the beginning herbalist a selection of eight or ten of the following will provide a good start: parsley, marjoram, chives, garlic chives, thyme, oregano, dill, lemon balm, bergamot (Oswego tea), mint, spearmint, peppermint, summer savory, European pennyroyal and sage.

Perhaps the easiest way to start from seed is to plant in flats in garden soil that has been pasteurized by being heated moist in an oven at about 200° F for half an hour. (A mixture of equal parts soil and peat is also good for this purpose.) Seed should be started six to eight weeks before the last expected frost, for early growth of most herbs is very slow.

Just before planting time, seeds of perennials (except those from the tropics) may be frozen and thawed several times to break dormancy. Annuals and biennials do not need this treatment.

Germination is often poor and the seedlings are usually very small so the seeds should be sown rather thickly. Cover the seeds lightly (about 1/10 inch) with soil, sand or milled peat and keep the germinating medium moist but not wet.

When the seedlings are well up, select a few of the strongest plants and transfer them to individual pots. Grow the plants in a sunny spot indoors or in a greenhouse or hotbed until warm weather has settled and then plant in their final locations.

Many gardeners purchase young plants, especially perennials. Excellent herb nurseries are scattered over the country and are worth a visit. (The smell inside an herb nursery is a delight and most nurserymen will allow you to pick off a leaf and taste and sniff before you buy.)

A few nurseries ship plants, so hundreds of varieties are available to the interested gardener, including many that are seldom or never available from seed. Only one or two plants or clumps of most herbs are needed, so the slight extra cost involved in shipping is usually well spent.

Soil Needs

Many herbs are from rather dry areas around the Mediterranean and seem adapted to poor soil and low moisture. Most writers on the subject mention that poor soil, in fact, is ideal for developing the oils which provide fragrance and taste of herbs. This may be true but all herbs will grow well on good garden soil and most of us would probably do well to grow them there at first and then experiment with some plant divisions in poorer soil.

Survival Gardening mounds are excellent for herbs. There is a problem, however. Many herbs are very invasive. For this reason you may prefer to grow them in pots which you may imbed in the ground. This will prevent their spreading. Having herbs potted has the added advantage that selected herbs, especially the most cold-sensitive ones, may be moved indoors in the winter.

Some Less-Usual Herbs and Spices for the Garden

Paprika is easily raised and is delicious used as a green frying-pepper or cut up in salads. The plants are rampant growers, some varieties growing as vines, and they produce profusely until frost. For a family, one or two plants will provide green peppers until nearly the first frost and then the last fruits may be allowed to mature. Pick when thoroughly red; cut open lengthwise and allow to dry completely. The pods may be stored "as is" or ground with or without the seed. (The resulting "paprika" is hotter if the seeds are used.)

Warning: An occasional pepper may be very hot. If you are especially sensitive to hot peppers, test with care.

Horseradish can become a rampant weed but if kept under control will add spice to dressings and sauces. Roots for planting are available by mail from several seed houses. The roots are used two ways. They can be cleaned and boiled like turnips or they may be ground and mixed with vinegar as is done to produce the commerical product.

Many herbs are used as teas. Some, such as mints, spearmint, peppermint, matte, clary sage and bergamot, make excellent tea when used alone. Most any mixture of the "tea herbs" makes a good tea, however.

If the fresh herbs are available, a handfull of leaves still on the cut stems will make a couple of cups. Dried teas are much stronger and a heaping teaspoonful is a good starting amount per cup. Put the leaves into boiling water and allow to steep while cooling. Most will develop their flavor in three to five minutes but some require longer.

Of the above teas, matte is the most unusual. It is a shrub or small tree — a holly — from South America which can be grown from seed. It is very sensitive to cold so must be brought in in the winter. One way to handle it is to set the plant out in the spring after all danger of frost has passed and grow it outside until frost is expected. Cut the shrub back to 6-8 inches high and reserve the leafy branches to let the leaves dry. Pot the shrub and keep near a window inside until spring.

Space Requirements and Typical Heights of Selected Culinary Herbs

	Herb	Space (ft.²)	Height (ft.)*	Comments
Annuals and biennials treated as annuals (Planted each year)	Anise	0.5	2	Biennial
	Basil	1	1-3	
	Borage	1.5	1-2	
	Caraway	0.3	2-3	
	Chamomile, German	0.5	2-3	
	Chervil	0.3	2	
	Coriander	0.3	1-2	Called Chinese Parsley
	Cumin	0.4	0.5	
	Dill	0.5	3-4	
	Fennel, Florence	1	4-5	
	Parsley	0.8	1	Biennial
	Purslane	1	0.5-1	Spreads
	Savory, summer	0.3	1-2	
Perennials (Remain in same space year after year)	Bay**	5-25	3-10	A shrub. Tender***
	Bergamot	1-2	3-4	Called Oswego tea
	Burnet	1.5	1-2	
	Chamomile, Roman	1	1	
	Chives	1	1-2	Divide each 2-3 years
	Garlic chives	1	1-2	Divide each 2-3 years
	Horseradish	3	2	Spreads
	Lemon balm	1-3	2-4	Spreads
	Lovage	6-8	3-7	
	Marjoram	1	1-2	Needs winter protection***
	Oregano	1-2	1-2	
	Peppermint	1	1-3	Spreads
	Pennyroyal, English	1	1	Spreads
	Rosemary	4-6	2-3	Needs winter protection***
	Sage	2	1-2	Spreads slowly
	Savory, winter	1	1	
	Sorrel, French	0.8	2-3	
	Spearmint	1.5	2-3	Spreads
	Tarragon	1.5	2	Needs winter protection***
	Thyme	0.3	0.5-1	Spreads
	Watercress	1	0.5-1	Spreads

*Dwarf or low - growing varieties of some herbs are available.

**Bay may be kept cut as a small shrub, even potted and brought indoors in winter.

***These herbs need winter protection, such as an extra heavy winter mulch, in areas where the temperature drops below about 20° F. (-7° C).

Some Culinary Uses of Herbs You Grow Yourself

	As vegetables	With meats	With fish	In soups, stews	In salads	Teas	Breads	Herb butter	Vinegars	
Angelica	St					L				
Anise				S	L					S in apple dishes
Applemint						L				
Basil	L		L	L	L			L	L	L in Italian dishes; tomatoes
Bay		L	L	L						
Bergamot						L				
Borage	L				L	L				Fl in beverages
Burnet					L			L	L	In soft cheeses
Caraway							S			S with apple, cabbage, mild cheeses
Cardoon	St			St	St					
Chamomile						Fl				
Chervil		L	L	L	L					L with eggs and vegetables
Chives		L	L	L	L		L	L		Onion substitute
Clary sage						L				
Coriander				L	L					S in pickling spices
Costmary		L			L	L				L with roast goose; in sausage
Cress	L				L					
Cumin		L	L	L	L					Indian and Mexican dishes
Dill		L	L		L		L, St.		Fl	In mild cheeses
Florence fennel	B		L, B		B					
French tarragon			L		L				L	L with eggs
Garlic				B	B			B		In sauces and dressings
Garlic chives		L	L	L	L			L		With various vegetables; as garlic
Horseradish	R									With vinegar as condiment
Lemon balm			L		L	L				In fruit salads
Lemon thyme			L	L	L	L				
Marjoram		L		L	L	L				
Matte'						L				
Mint						L	L			L with lamb; in jellies
Nasturtium					L, Fl					Immature fruit pickled
Onion seed		S	S	S						In Indian dishes
Oregano		L	L	L	L			L		In Italian and Greek dishes
Paprika	Fr	Fr		Fr	Fr					Green fruit fried
Parsley		L	L	L	L					As garnish
Pennyroyal						L				
Peppermint						L	L			L with fresh fruit
Purslane	L, St.			L, St.						Stir-fry as vegetable
Rosemary		L	L	L	L	L	L			L in stuffings
Sage										With pork, poultry, soft cheeses
Savory		L			L					In pork and poultry stuffing
Sorrel	L			L	L					
Spearmint			L		L	L				L with fresh fruit
Thyme		L	L	L	L				L	

KEY: B = bulb or bulb-like structure; Fl = flower; Fr = fruit; L = leaves; R = root; S = seed; St = stem.

Economics of Home Gardening ...

CHAPTER FOURTEEN

Aside from gardening methods and the vagaries of weather, which do provide for great uncertainties in the economics of gardening, most people really know little about the costs or profits from their gardening efforts. This chapter is to help you make economic choices about what to grow on a more realistic basis though, for obvious reasons, a high degree of personal judgment is called for.

If you are gardening to lower your food costs — one of the main reasons for gardening in many families — you should study carefully the tables in this chapter and consider this strategy.

Select vegetables you and your family use that do grow well in your area. Then prepare your own table like the one at the left listing these vegetables in the first vertical column. In the second column insert the expected yield per 25 square feet per week using the data in the table on Nutrient Yields in Intensive Gardening (pp. 64-66). This figure is determined by dividing "Lbs. per 25 sq. ft." (col. 3) by "Weeks from planting through harvest" (col. 2). Then estimate from your experience (or use last year's newspapers) to determine expected average price per pound of each vegetable, and insert this figure in column 3.

Multiply the figures in columns 2 and 3 to obtain estimated dollar yields per 25 square feet per week and insert this in column 4.

The figures in column 4 will provide estimates of relative savings to be realized for a given area of growing space each week it is used for these crops. A decision to grow crops giving the highest savings will generally be most advantageous, especially if the space is used throughout the gardening season.

Your production costs will be about the same, so have little effect on relative savings.

How-to Charts on Economics of Gardening

A. Illustrative Estimates of Relative Income or Savings Weekly per 25 Square Feet for Selected Garden Crops.

Crop	Yield/25 sq. ft./week (lb.)	Price ($/lb.)	Relative Value/Week ($)
Tomato	3.1	0.50	1.55
Potato	5.6	0.20	1.12
Squash, yellow	1.9	0.45	0.86
Zucchini	7.3	0.50	3.65
Peppers, green	0.78	0.60	0.47
Lettuce, leaf	5.1	0.60	3.06
Muskmelon	1.1	0.50	0.55

B. Illustration of How to Calculate Areas for Your Selected Crops

Crop	(A)* Yield/25 sq. ft. (lbs.)	(B) Desired Yield (lbs.)	Area to Plant** (sq. ft.)
Zucchini	80	20	6
Tomato	49	50	26
Lettuce	51	10	5
Potato	50	50	25

*Figures for yield should be adjusted for local experience to reflect variations from area to area and the differences of efficiency of gardeners.

**Area to be planted $= \dfrac{B}{A} \times 25$

Any family may find the yield of a particular crop from 25 square feet (about the area of four card tables) too great or too small for its needs. To optimize use of space, estimate the amounts needed of the desired vegetables and, using the yield per crop (column 3, pp. 64-66), calculate the area to be devoted to each as illustrated in table B on the preceding page.

In this illustration, a single hill of zucchini would probably meet the needs of a family but it would occupy more than the allotted six square feet.

This may be a good time for you to consider "enlarging" your garden by companion planting which almost invariably increases the total yield per unit space. Considering only the four vegetables in the example given, all the lettuce you and your family can eat, plus some to give friends, could be grown and partially harvested before the zucchini is planted. Lettuce could also be planted among the tomato and potato plants where it has the added advantage of being an excellent cover crop.

For many gardeners the method will need modification because, for one reason or another, they abandon some crops before production stops.

To make this adjustment, you can develop a table as shown on this page. List the crops being considered in the first column, the yield per 25 square feet (from pp. 64-66) in the next column, the estimated price per pound in the third and total crop value in the fourth column. Estimate the fraction of the crop to be harvested and insert this in the fifth column. Multiply the figures for each crop and insert this figure in the final column, Value of Harvest.

A comparison of charts A and C is instructive. There are some differences in relative savings if the **whole** season is to be used as contrasted with the savings per **week**. Also if only part of the harvest is gathered and is used, there are quite significant differences in your savings. Most of the work and expense has been applied to the garden by the time the harvest is half done. Abandonment at this date often happens and is a real loss in time for the rest of the harvest is almost "for free".

Gardeners who wish to estimate relative earnings from different crops can use the same method except that it is not necessary to decide how much the family needs.

C. Estimate of Value of Harvest per 25 Sq. Ft. When Garden Is Only Partly Harvested

Crop	Yield/25 sq. ft. (lbs.)	Price/lb. ($)	Value Total ($)	Fraction Harvested	Value of Harvest ($)
Tomato	49	0.50	24.50	0.75	18.38
Potato	50	0.20	10.00	1.00	10.00
Squash, yellow	19	0.45	8.55	0.75	6.41
Zucchini	80	0.50	40.00	0.75	30.00
Peppers, green	21	0.60	12.60	0.80	11.80
Lettuce, leaf	51	0.60	30.60	0.95	29.07
Muskmelon	18	0.50	9.00	1.00	9.00

A Matter of Life ...

Some personal comments

*We need to prepare for
a surprise-full future
and plan accordingly
for resilience in dealing
with these surprises.*
L. Hunter Lovins

CHAPTER FIFTEEN

Survival Gardening is based on the idea that in the not too distant future it may be essential that many more people know how to produce a very high proportion of their own food. It is possible that some communities will have to produce all they eat. We can hope if such a time does come it will arrive slowly enough that adjustments will already have been made to survive.

But what if we are cut off from all outside resources through a sudden, lasting reduction in fuel supplies or a global disintegration of the economic system, or through the isolation of war?

Obviously, such an extreme situation would mean everyone would be forced to make drastic changes in lifestyle. However, it is the crucial area of food — its production, harvesting and home storage — that I try to deal with in *Survival Gardening*.

How do I think I would further adjust my own current gardening methods in order to have, in the most literal sense, a Survival Garden?

One thing is sure. I would as quickly as possible increase my garden production in quantity and nutritive quality. One aspect of increasing probable productivity would involve my looking about for additional and previously unused resources.

My most immediately available resource is additional space. For several years now, I have kept one to three optional garden sites in readiness for future use. They have been heavily mulched to reduce weed growth and to enrich the soil. The oldest one (three years) was used once during this period for a bumper crop of tomatoes when I had a number of plants but insufficient garden space because other plants were producing longer than expected. These areas can be planted with a minimum of additional preparation at the appropriate season and in each case the soil is potentially very productive.

The creek and several springs on our property could be our emergency source of water, hand-pumped, to house or garden.

In our particular situation, I would prepare another garden or several gardens in the floodplain across the creek from our house to improve the chances we would have at least one productive garden in case of a drought. If I had enough warning time, this would involve cutting down the trees for firewood. If time were at a great premium, I would simply girdle the trees and let them stand defoliated throughout the garden.

I would develop further the methods I already use for getting the greatest number of plants from the seeds I use by germinating them before planting.

In Asia, especially, human wastes are valued as fertilizers. These, along with sludge from domestic septic tanks, may be used safely if buried under eight to ten inches of soil. In areas where I grow crops in which the edible part is never in contact with the soil, I would start using both. At the same time, I would look around for other neglected fertilizers that could improve new garden areas. These might include decayed sawdust and logs, cotton seed wastes, and a host of other compostable materials.

I would develop a more efficient system for having transplants right ready to insert in places being deserted as plants are harvested. In Africa I saw gardens that looked as though each vacated space was immediately planted. I would try this more faithfully than I have done in the past.

I would arrange our plumbing, if practical, so that greywater from kitchen and bath could be used as appropriate for irrigation. I would arrange to divert water from roof to garden so that a small rain in the summer would have a doubled effect.

I would immediately place greater emphasis on growing the "Very Special Survival Vegetables" so we would get the maximum nutrition from the space being gardened.

I would change my method of harvesting some plants, e.g., pinching off the outer leaves of spinach rather than cutting off the whole plant. Another quick change would be to use even more of our produce than at present. If my wife did not already do much of this, we would start using the tender peelings of white potatoes and sweetpotatoes, the core of cabbage, the leaves of kohlrabi and the outer leaves of lettuce. Beet greens are more nutritious than the root, so I think we would quickly adapt our taste buds to the use of beet greens in some way. More leaves of broccoli might well be added to our diet. We would continue to remove only the receptacle of okra rather than throwing away part of the edible fruit and use the interior of vitamin-rich peppers, which we already consider one of our prime and most versatile vegetables.

We would search out more of the wild plants we now use to a limited extent. "Poke salad" would appear more often on our table. (We have several large clumps and find we can eat the *young* leaves in both spring and summer.) We would take advantage of our edible daylilies and the Jerusalem artichokes that are largely uncollected. We would use lamb's quarter as a boiled green rather than simply as a mulch.

We would increase the number of winter-stored plants such as beets, rutabaga, salsify, parsnips.

Of course, I can only estimate how much effect these changes would have. Except for the increased space, I expect the effect would be overall to increase at least several-fold the total nutrients from our garden, especially because of the emphasis we would put on growing and using the Very Special Survival Vegetables. (I consider these V.S.S.V. important enough to devote the first chapter to them!)

Regardless of whether the future brings widespread disruptions, an increased degree of family and local self-sufficiency is needed. In our world in which we are already overusing many of our resources, such a development will extend the resources we have and also reduce the shocks when shortages or disruptions do occur.

Many people doing some form of Survival Gardening could well serve as the catalyst to bring people together into communities. Ties of interdependence would develop far beyond the sharing of gardening space, tools, produce and labor. Such ties are able to support all sorts of projects which under favorable circumstances tend to make the community a good place to live. Under catastrophic circumstances, such ties may well be the difference between a community's disintegration and its survival.

J.A.F.

The Survival Gardener's Library

A. The World Food Situation

Gabel, M. *HO-PING: Food for Everyone.* Anchor Books (Doubleday), Garden City, N.Y.

Lappe, Frances M., and J. Collins. *Food First.* Houghton Mifflin, Boston.

Merrill, R. (ed). *Radical Agriculture.* Harper & Row, New York.

Pimental, David and Marcia. *Food, Energy and Society.* Edward Arnold, London.

B. Gardening

Anon. *Guide to almost Foolproof Gardening.* Mother Earth News, Hendersonville, N.C.

Chan, Peter. *Better Vegetable Gardens the Chinese Way.* Graphic Arts Center, Portland, Oregon.

Jeavons, J. *How to Grow More Vegetables . . .* Ten Speed Press, Box 7123, Berkeley, Ca. 94707.

Rodale, J.I., ed. *How To Grow Vegetables and Fruits by the Organic Method.* Rodale Press, Emmaus, Pa.

Seymour, J. *The Self-Sufficient Gardener.* Faber & Faber, London. 1978.

Staff of Organic Gardening Magazine. *The Encyclopedia of Organic Gardening.* Rodale Press, Emmaus, Pa.

Yepsen, R.B., Jr. *Organic Plant Protection.* Rodale Press, Emmaus, Pa.

C. Soil

Handbook on Soils. Brooklyn Botanical Garden, New York.

Hyams, E. *Soil and Civilization.* Harper and Row, New York. 1976. (Reprint; originally published in 1952).

Logsdon, G. *The Gardener's Guide to Better Soil.* Rodale Press, Emmaus, Pa.

D. Fruits and Nuts

Clarke, J.H. *Growing Berries and Grapes at Home.* Dover, New York.

Hedrick, U.P. *Fruits for the Home Garden.* Dover, New York.

Riotte, Louise. *Nuts for the Home Gardener.* Garden Way, Charlotte, Vt.

Smith, J.R. *Tree Crops: A Permanent Agriculture.* Harper and Row, New York.

E. Home Food Storage

Loveday, Evelyn V., *Complete Book of Home Storage of Vegetables and Fruits.* Garden Way, Charlotte, Vt.

Stoner, Carol H. (ed.) *Stocking Up.* Rodale Press, Emmaus, Pa.

continued

F. Miscellaneous Books

Anon. *Report and Recommendations on Organic Farming*. U.S.D.A., Washington

Howard, Sir Albert. *An Agricultural Testament*. Rodale Press, Emmaus, Pa.

Hylton, William H. (ed.). *The Rodale Herb Book*. Rodale Press, Emmaus, Pa.

Johnston, R. *Growing Garden Seeds: A Manual for Gardeners and Small Farmers*. Johnny's Selected Seeds, Albion, Maine.

King, F.H. *Farmers For Forty Centuries*. Rodale Press, Emmaus, Pa.

Lorenz, O.A., and D.N. Maynard. *Knott's Handbook for Vegetable Growers*. Wiley-Interscience, New York.

McCullagh, J.C. *The Solar Greenhouse Book*. Rodale Press, Emmaus, Pa.

Melillo, J.M. *Ecology Primer*. Pendulum Press, New Haven, Conn.

Morse, R.A. *The Complete Guide to Beekeeping*. Dutton, New York.

Philbrick, Helen and John. *The Bug Book*. Garden Way, Charlotte, Vt.

Picart, F. *Escargots From Your Garden To Your Table*. F. Picart Snails, 1550 Ridley Ave., Santa Rosa, Ca.

Root, A.I. *ABC and XYZ of Beeculture*. A.I. Root, Box 706, Medina, OH

Sammataro, Diana and A. Avitabile. *The Beekeeper's Handbook*. Peach Mountain Press, Dexter, Mich.

Stevens, J.T., *Making the Best of Basics -- Family Preparedness Handbook*. Peton Corp., Salt Lake City, Ut.

U.S.D.A. Agricultural Handbook No. 512, *The Basic Principles of Insect Population Suppression and Management*. U.S. Govt. Printing Office, Washington, D.C. 20402

Watt, B.K., and A.L. Merrill, *Handbook of the Nutritional Contents of Foods*. Dover, New York. (U.S.D.A. Handbook #8)

We did not inherit the earth from our parents, we are borrowing it from our children.

Author unknown

INDEX

Individual vegetables appear in the tables but are not indexed except for the Very Special Survival Vegetables and certain others which provide exceptionally high yields of one or more nutrients.

Key: Bold -- Major reference; *Italics* -- Table or illustration; Regular type -- Minor reference

Photograph of the author taken on a windy day by Andy Burriss, **Rock Hill Evening Herald**

*One hopeful sign I see
for the future is
the growing interest
in gardening today
by people who show
in their own backyards
an awareness of
the distinction between
use and misuse
of the only Earth
we have.*

Our task must be to free ourselves . . . by widening our circle of compassion to embrace all living creatures and the whole nature in its beauty.

Albert Einstein